THE
ATLANTIS
ENIGMA

By the same author
Ancient Spirit
Aquarian Guide to the New Age (with Eileen Campbell)
Astral Doorways
Discover Astral Projection
Discover Reincarnation
Experimental Magic
Getting Rich: A Beginner's Manual
A Guide to Megalithic Ireland
How to Get Where You Want to Go
Magick for Beginners
Martian Genesis
Mindreach
Nostradamus – Visions of the Future
An Occult History of the World
Occult Reich
Reincarnation
Time Travel: A New Perspective
The Ultimate Elsewhere

Find out more about the author and his books by visiting
Herbie Brennan's Bookshelf on the World Wide Web:
http://homepage.tinet.ie./~herbie

Note

All measurements used in this book are imperial.
To find the metric equivalent use the table below:

1 inch	=	2.54 centimetres
1 foot	=	0.3048 metre
1 yard	=	0.9144 metre
1 mile	=	1.6903 kilometres
1 acre	=	0.4047 hectare
1 square mile	=	2.59 square kilometres
1 cubic yard	=	0.7646 cubic metre
1 ton (metric)	=	1,000 kilograms

THE
ATLANTIS
ENIGMA

HERBIE BRENNAN

PIATKUS

Dedication
For June, who sent me searching for Atlantis years ago ...
... and for the team at Freeverse Software whose fine
computer games kept me sane while I was doing the
research.

© 1999 Herbie Brennan

First published in 1999 by
Judy Piatkus (Publishers) Ltd
5 Windmill Street, London W1P 1HF

The right of Herbie Brennan to be identified as Author of this Work
has been asserted by him in accordance with the Copyright, Designs
and Patents Act 1988

A catalogue record for this book is available from the British Library

ISBN 0–7499–1965–5

Edited by John Malam
Designed by Sue Ryall

Set in Garamond

Typeset by Wyvern 21, Bristol
Printed and bound in Great Britain by
Butler & Tanner, Frome, Somerset

CONTENTS

1   SEARCH FOR ATLANTIS   1
2   PLATO'S DESCRIPTION   11
3   AMERICAN EVIDENCE   19
4   MYSTERIES IN EGYPT   28
5   ASTOUNDING DISCOVERIES   39
6   ANCIENT MARINERS   50
7   PREHISTORIC PUZZLE   58
8   CRACKS IN THE CONSENSUS   67
9   THE ICE AGE MYTH   76
10 GLOBAL CATACLYSM   84
11 QUAKES AND VOLCANOES   93
12 CHANGING CLIMATE   106
13 THE OUTER SPACE CONNECTION   116
14 ASTEROIDS AND COMETS   125
15 MISSING PLANET   131
16 DEVASTATED SOLAR SYSTEM   140
17 SUPERNOVA FRAGMENT   148
18 WAR IN HEAVEN   158
19 COSMIC BOMBARDMENT   167
20 DELUGE AND FLOOD   177
21 AFTERMATH OF DISASTER   185

    EPILOGUE   193
    INDEX   201

1
SEARCH FOR ATLANTIS

FACT

YOU WOULD HAVE TO DESTROY A WHOLE SCIENTIFIC
PARADIGM BEFORE YOU COULD BELIEVE IN ANYTHING
AS FANCIFUL AS PLATO'S LOST ATLANTIS.

In December 1997, the Russian scholar Viatcheslav Koudriavtsev applied to the UK Foreign Office for permission to conduct an underwater archaeological survey of Little Sole Bank, a site 165 feet deep, some 100 miles off the Cornish coast of south-west Britain. Koudriavtsev, who planned to lead a twenty-strong expedition of divers, marine cartographers and engineers, was supported by the prestigious Russian Academy of Sciences. His interest in Little Sole was unusual for a well-respected academic. He believed it used to be the capital of Atlantis.

As Koudriavtsev finalised his plans for Little Sole, the English explorer Colonel John Blashford-Snell prepared his own expedition to Atlantis. He was convinced it had been sited on an island destroyed millennia ago by volcanic action, in Bolivia's Lake Poopo.

This sort of disagreement is by no means unusual. The American scholar Ignatius Donnelly placed Atlantis in the Atlantic, as did Madame H. P. Blavatsky, the founder of Theosophy, whose Secret Masters told her that it sank in stages. The official *Guide to Kerry* mentions blandly that the Aran Islands, off Ireland's west coast, once formed part of Atlantis. Other traditions suggest it actually encompassed the whole of Ireland, but not the remainder of the British Isles, which were then attached to Europe.

Journalist and author Lewis Spence tended to believe it lay off the coast of Africa, and may even have been attached to it at one time. Architect H. R. Stahel illustrated it as a chain of islands stretching from Newfoundland in a more or less straight line towards Spain.

Dr John Dee, the Court Astrologer to Queen Elizabeth I, was convinced the newly discovered North American continent was Atlantis, and labelled it as such on one of his maps. This view was shared by Francis Bacon – who saw South America as a possibility as well – and several other scholars of the time.

Archaeologists Angelos Galanopoulos and Spiridon Marinatos concluded that the story of Atlantis represented distorted memories of Minoan Crete. The attraction was their belief that the violent volcanic eruption which destroyed the island of Thera, some time around 1500 BC, caused the collapse of the Minoan civilisation. Despite discrepancies with the original tradition (you have to divide by ten to make the dates fit, for example) the theory was championed by the Dublin scholar Professor J. V. Luce.[1]

---

[1] But the idea is less popular than it once was. Recent geological discoveries now suggest the Thera eruption did *not* coincide with the decline of the Minoan civilisation.

The habit of juggling the figures to make new theories fit traditional accounts was not confined to Galanopoulos, Marinatos and Luce. The German geographer Albert Hermann divided the supposed size of Atlantis by thirty in order to locate it in the Shott el Djerid, a dried-up marsh in Tunisia.

In 1953, a diving expedition led by the German Jurgen Spanuth, discovered rock walls at a depth of 45 feet near Heligoland, a rocky island in the North Sea, which he promptly claimed were remnants of Atlantis.

Adolf Schulten is among the archaeologists who have suggested an ancient Tartessian culture stretched from southern Spain into Morocco via islands in the Straits of Gibraltar now drowned by the Mediterranean. This culture, they say, was Atlantis – or at least an Atlantean colony.

Atlantis was in Nigeria, according to the archaeologist Leo Frobenius, who was impressed by the similarities between Olokun, the Yoruba god of the ocean, and Poseidon, the divine founder of Atlantis.

In 1925, the explorer Colonel P. H. Fawcett, set off into the Brazilian jungle hoping to find traces of Atlantis there, but never returned to say whether or not he had succeeded.

According to author Charles Berlitz, Atlantis has variously been placed in Portugal, France, England, Sweden, Belgium, Prussia, Italy, Spitsbergen, Iran, Ceylon (Sri Lanka), the Caucasus mountains, Russia's Azov Sea and a submarine location off the coast of Holland.

Even Edgar Cayce, America's famous 'sleeping prophet' got in on the act. Cayce, who died in 1945, achieved a fearsome reputation as a healer, and made diagnoses and prescriptions while in a self-induced hypnotic trance. Eventually he began to prophesy, predicting that Atlantis would rise from the depths in 1968 or '69. Enthusiastic followers waited in vain for the lost continent to reappear. Many consoled themselves with the fact that American archaeologist Dr Manson Valentine had discovered an impressive underwater wall, west of Bimini in the Bahamas, during 1968.

More recently, Rand and Rose Flem-Ath published an extraordinarily persuasive hypothesis equating Atlantis with the Antarctic continent. According to this theory, the lost civilisation now lies buried under ice – and the land of its birth never sank beneath the waves at all.[2]

The Greek philosopher Plato, who launched the story of Atlantis, placed it 'beyond the Pillars of Hercules', a term generally taken to denote the Straits of Gibraltar. This loose location means it could have been almost anywhere, except in the Mediterranean.

What Plato described was 'a great power which advanced from its base in the Atlantic Ocean to attack the cities of Europe and Asia'. In those days, he wrote, the Atlantic was navigable. Opposite the Straits of Gibraltar was an island larger than Libya and Asia put together. From it, sailors could reach other islands, leading eventually to the 'whole opposite continent which surrounds . . . the ocean'.[3]

This passage isn't entirely clear. First, the term 'larger than Libya and Asia' is deceptive. What was understood as Asia, in Plato's day, is a far cry from the landmass we now call Asia. And 'Libya' wasn't modern Libya either, but rather a loose definition of North Africa excluding Egypt. All the same, the island opposite the Straits was obviously very large and might even deserve the term 'continent' applied to it by so many later writers. The

---

[2] *When the Sky Fell*, Orion Books, London, 1996.

[3] In his *Timeaus*. The extracts are from the Desmond Lee translation, Penguin Classics, London, 1971.

'whole opposite continent' surrounding the Atlantic Ocean is less easy to understand. If the term refers to anything at all, the most likely candidate is the Americas which don't, of course, surround the Atlantic, but are quite big enough for early sailors to suppose they did.

What you have then, are the Americas on one side of the Atlantic, a huge oceanic island quite close to the Straits of Gibraltar, and a chain of lesser islands between them. It was the huge oceanic island that Plato called Atlantis.

Plato's term 'those days' is easier to interpret, providing we're not too concerned with pinpoint accuracy. The Egyptian priests from whom Plato had the story, via his ancestor Solon, claimed Athens was founded 9,000 years earlier, although elsewhere Plato assigned this date to the Atlantean attack. Since we know the year of Solon's journey to Egypt, we can calculate that Atlantis was still above water and causing trouble sometime around 9600 BC.

The trouble was considerable. Atlantis was ruled by a dynasty of kings whose military prowess had enabled them to take over many of the islands in the trans-Atlantic chain and parts of the American mainland. They also had control of Libya (that is, tracts of North Africa) up to the borders with Egypt, and tracts of Europe as far as Tyrrhenia, a land that once encompassed Corsica, Sardinia and parts of Italy.

But despite these extensive colonies, the Atlanteans still wanted more. They launched an attack on 'all the territory within the strait', obviously with ambitions to control the entire Mediterranean. They might have managed it too, had it not been for Athens. When the Atlanteans attacked, the city-state of Athens led an alliance of Greeks against them. At first, things went badly for the defenders. The alliance collapsed, but Athens continued to fight alone and eventually pushed back the Atlantean troops, ensuring the freedom of the Mediterranean states.

At some point after this war – if the Egyptians specified how long, Plato does not report it – there came a time of extraordinarily violent earthquakes and floods. Athens took enormous damage: according to Plato, her armies were 'swallowed up by the earth'. Atlantis fared even worse. The entire island was inundated by the sea 'in a single dreadful day and night'.

The story so far has been taken from Plato's *Timaeus*, but he returned to it again in a later work called *Critias*, which contains a vivid description of the Atlantean civilisation. While recapping on the war and its catastrophic aftermath, he described Atlantis as having been 'overwhelmed by earthquakes' to become the source of the mud that impeded free passage from the Straits of Gibraltar into the open sea. This suggests an Atlantic location of Atlantis, very close to the mouth of the Mediterranean.

But wherever Plato may have put his island continent, modern historians take his story as an allegory or outright myth. Atlantis simply doesn't fit into prehistory as we know it.

The earliest creatures identified as ancestors of modern humanity are known as *Australopithecus*, a term that means 'southern apes'. They roamed in south and east Africa about 3 million years ago. They were small and decidedly simian, but they walked upright and fashioned simple tools from stone and bone. In short, they had potential.

That potential seems to have resulted in *Homo habilis* ('Handy Man') and *Homo erectus* ('Upright Man') around the beginning of the Pleistocene, some 2.5 million years ago.

There is some gentle controversy here. Perhaps *Australopithecus* evolved into *Habilis* who evolved into *Erectus*. Or perhaps *Habilis* didn't evolve into *Erectus*. Or perhaps *Pithecus* didn't directly evolve into either. Perhaps there were several parallel strains. No matter. The important thing is that at a certain stage, *Erectus* evolved into *Homo sapiens* ('Wise Man'), the self-congratulatory label scientists have applied to our own species. It happened in Africa and it happened somewhere between 400,000 and 100,000 years ago. Either date places the appearance of humanity in the Ice Age.

In 1856, the remains of several peculiar people were discovered in Germany's Neander Valley. At once the experts began to argue whether these were the bones of early humans, or just the bones of modern humans distorted by disease. The controversy was settled when similar skeletons were unearthed elsewhere. Neanderthals were definitely early humans. It transpired that they had lived throughout Europe, the Mediterranean, North Africa, the Middle East and parts of central Asia between about 100,000 and 35,000 years ago.

Nobody quite knows where Neanderthals came from. All we know is that they lived, used tools, buried their dead with flowers, and probably practised some form of religion. We also know they disappeared.

Cro-Magnon is the name of a rock shelter near Les Eyzies-de-Tayac, in the Dordogne region of France. In 1868, geologist Louis Lartet was digging there when he discovered human remains dating to the Upper Palaeolithic (35,000 to 10,000 years ago). There were the bones of more than ten people in the shelter, but for some reason only five were preserved for archaeological investigation. They were impressive specimens, varying in height from 5 feet 5 inches to 6 feet 3 inches. There was every indication they had been strong-jawed and firm-muscled, and their skulls had the capacity to house large brains. One of them had attained the age of fifty, a remarkable feat for the time.[4]

In 1882, the French prehistorians, A. de Quatrefages and Ernest Hamy, decided that Cro-Magnons represented a specific branch of the human race. Experts now believe they originated in western Asia.

It's clear that Cro-Magnons and Neanderthals overlapped. It's not clear whether genocide or interbreeding caused the Neanderthal strain to disappear, but it was Cro-Magnon who survived. Cro-Magnons were *Homo sapiens sapiens* ('Wise, Wise Man'). Cro-Magnons were us. To this day, there are people in Sweden and the Canary Islands who seem to be of almost unadulterated Cro-Magnon stock.

About 13,000 years ago, the world at last began to warm. It didn't warm everywhere and it didn't warm all at once – the final remnants of a great North American ice sheet took a further 5,500 years to thaw – but it was clear at some point in the process that the Ice Age was drawing to a close. Scientists usually put the cut-off date around 8000 BC, a time that marked the final fragmentation of a dwindling Scandinavian ice sheet.

The melting of the ice brought about a major rise in world sea levels. Although higher than they used to be, by 8000 BC they were still about 110 feet lower than they are today. But they rose until about 4000 BC, at which time they stabilised.

This development changed the geography of the planet. Large tracts of land simply disappeared under water to become what we now call 'continental shelves'. The land bridge across the Bering

---

[4] Even today, fifty remains the life expectancy of the average Egyptian.

Strait, from Asia to Alaska, disappeared. So did the connections between the British Isles and Europe, Japan and Siberia, Sri Lanka and India, and Tasmania and Australia. For the first time in millennia, pockets of human population found themselves isolated.

There was a widespread change in vegetation. In western Europe, the sparse growths of the former tundra were first replaced by forests of birch and pine, then of oak, elm, and hazel. Until about 3000 BC, world temperatures were generally 2°C to 3°C higher than the present day. It was a good time to start farming.

There is agreement among scientists that for most of the Pleistocene Ice Age, mankind lived as hunter-gatherers. If we extrapolate from observations of primitive tribal peoples today, this probably meant that the women were responsible for 80 to 85 per cent of the food supply, scavenged from anywhere they could find it, while once every two weeks or so the men would take themselves off to catch a little protein on the hoof.

Somewhere along the evolutionary process, it's likely that a percentage of these hunter-gatherers became nomadic herdsmen. A few prey species, like reindeer, were more or less domesticated.

But with the ending of the Ice Age, a major change took place. Humanity began to develop agriculture. As world temperatures rose, the successful cultivation of rice, wheat, barley, potatoes and maize became not only possible, but comparatively easy. Earlier preoccupations, like hunting, for example, diminished. Agriculture provided the food necessary for an increased population and led inevitably to a more settled lifestyle. People began to live in permanent houses. Tools grew more sophisticated. The gradual increase of barter laid the foundations of trade.

By the seventh millennium BC, villages were becoming more numerous in the Near East. Agriculture diversified. In the village of Jarmo, in Iraq, people learned how to domesticate pigs. Elsewhere, the storage of food became, like the tools needed to grow it, more sophisticated. Pit silos and granaries, some of them surprisingly large, were built. Crop irrigation was developed. The benefits of crop rotation were discovered.

Sometime between 4500 and 4000 BC, a non-Semitic people known as the Ubaidians settled in the southernmost part of Mesopotamia, between the two great rivers, Tigris and Euphrates, in what is now part of modern Iraq. They drained the marshes and began to plant crops. They developed trade with neighbouring tribes. They established industries such as weaving, leather-work, masonry and pottery. Their presence acted like a magnet. A number of Semitic peoples moved into the territory and a blending of cultures took place. The Sumerians, whose language was eventually adopted throughout the whole region, probably originated in Anatolia, Turkey. Their arrival about 3300 BC gave a name to the most exciting development of all – civilisation. By the third millennium BC, at least twelve separate city-states had arisen.

Sumer, with its walled cities, its agricultural hinterland and its increasing prosperity was the first known civilisation. Others followed in Egypt, Assyria, Greece and Rome. Humankind had emerged from the dark night of the Ice Age and was now firmly established on the long march to the Industrial Revolution, the internal combustion engine, the global economy, space exploration and the information age.

Scientists see it all as a linear progression, an inevitable evolution from the simple to the complex, from the crude to the sophisticated, from the coarse to the refined, from ignorance to understanding.

You would have to destroy a whole scientific paradigm before you could believe in anything as fanciful as Plato's lost Atlantis.

2

PLATO'S DESCRIPTION

_____ F A C T _____

ORTHODOXY CLAIMS THERE IS SCARCELY A WORD OF
PLATO'S LONG DESCRIPTION OF ATLANTIS AND ITS
CULTURE THAT COULD POSSIBLY BE TRUE.
_____

In 1969, archaeologists discovered twelve fossil footprints between Woolongong and Gerringong, Australia. The prints are 1 million years old.

In 1997, thermoluminescence dating techniques, applied to human artefacts discovered at the Jinmium site in Australia's Northern Territories, produced dates of 116,000 and 176,000 years BP (before Pleistocene). The findings were promptly disputed by scientists brought up to believe that modern man only appeared around 100,000 BP and even then was strictly confined to Africa. Although it was widely accepted that the Jinmium finds related to modern man, they simply couldn't be as old as 116,000 years (let alone 176,000). The geochronologist R. Roberts suggested their actual age was 10,000 years.

The Australian finds were not the first evidence to suggest modern humanity has been wandering this planet longer than the scientists allow. In 1970, for example, construction workers on a dam near Demirkopru, in Turkey, discovered a set of human footprints pressed into volcanic ash. One is now on display at the Natural History Museum in Stockholm, Sweden. Best estimates place it at 250,000 years old.

In 1928, an entire human skeleton unearthed at Ipswich, England, seemed to bear a minimum date of 330,000 years. A human jaw and some paleoliths of similar antiquity were discovered in the same year at Moulin Quignon, in France. The finds reinforced the much earlier discovery (in 1868) of a 330,000-year-old partial human skeleton at Clichy. The orthodox consensus dismissed the remains as forgeries and hoaxes.

The orthodox consensus has largely ignored the 600,000-year-old neoliths discovered at Gehe, China, in 1989 and the human femurs from Trimil in Java, found in 1973 and dated at 830,000 years BP. It has also ignored finds in Siberia, England, France and Italy which indicate human habitation of those countries prior to 1 million years BP, the time most orthodox scientists believe the first hominid (*Homo erectus*) had only just started thinking seriously about leaving Africa. Worse still for the orthodox consensus, England, Belgium, India, Pakistan and Italy are just a few of the countries that have yielded up implements in strata older than the 2 million years assigned to the evolution of *Homo habilis*, the first tool-user. *Habilis* was, in any case, supposed never to have left his native Africa.

But however many such finds appear – and the few mentioned are just the very small tip of a very large iceberg – they do not shake the paradigm of a linear evolution. They only suggest it started sooner than we thought.

The archaeological term 'tanged point complex' refers to something of a prehistoric mystery – the sudden appearance, in the ninth millennium BC, of a wholly new type of arrowhead. These arrowheads have been found in astonishingly large quantities along the coast of north-west Europe and the Near East. Nobody knows where they came from.

By a curious coincidence, burial sites of this era begin, for the first time, to show signs of violent death. Earlier burials sometimes yield up broken bones, but with no indication that these were anything but accidental. In the Djebel Sahaba excavation, by contrast, fifty-nine burials have accompanying arrowheads lodged in the rib-cages, spines and other bones. The same pattern appears in the forty-four excavated graves at the Vasylivka III site on the Dnieper River. Clearly those burials, and others like them, are warrior graves.

Rock paintings in the Spanish Levant, that area of the country fringing the Mediterranean, differ from earlier Magdalenian art in that they depict human figures in preference to animals. But not just any figures. Again and again these paintings, which date to the ninth millennium BC, depict bowmen in the heat of battle.

Putting the available evidence together, it would appear that humanity had at long last discovered the pleasures of war . . . at just about the time Plato claimed Atlantis launched its great invasion.

Of course, a great prehistoric war involving cave-dwelling bowmen, using flint arrowheads, doesn't exactly tally with Plato's description of an advanced civilisation on Atlantis – nor, indeed, with his description of the Athens which defeated it. He gives this description in his *Critias*, where, having discussed a mythical time when the gods divided Earth between them, he tells of the Athenians as comprising various classes of citizenry, some of whom were concerned with manufacturing while others were engaged in agriculture. There was a separate military class composed of men and women, both of whom engaged in regular military exercises and wore full armour. The various classes and occupations had their own living quarters, built using timber and stone. On the slopes of what later became the Acropolis, lived the craftsmen and farmers who worked in the neighbourhood. Higher up was a temple of Athena surrounded by a single wall. Within this enclosure lived a standing army of 20,000. Their homes, gymnasia and winter mess-rooms were on the northern side, although in summer they tended to move to the southern side where they may have spent most of their time in the open. This military establishment was the acknowledged leader not only of Athens, but of Greece as a whole and was widely admired throughout Europe and Asia.

This interesting fantasy conflicts directly with what the archaeologists have told us about prehistoric Greece. At the time of which Plato spoke, the world was still in the grip of the Ice Age. Agriculture had not yet developed, let alone the advanced concept of manufacturing. Nobody wore armour or lived in houses. The most advanced form of dwelling was the cave. The first stone temple to Athena on the Acropolis was not built until 580 BC, more than 9,000 years after the time Plato was describing. Before then, the best Greece had to offer was a few primitive mud-brick shrines.

But if Plato was off target with his description of prehistoric Greece, he was almost off the planet when he started to describe Atlantis.

Atlantis, claimed Plato, comprised a broad plain with a low central hill enclosed by concentric rings of water and land. In the centre were two springs, one cold, one hot, suggesting volcanic action. The island's soil was exceptionally fertile. It produced extensive forests and supported an abundance of wildlife, notably elephants.

Politically, the island was divided into ten territories, each under the rule of its own king. The territories seemed to hold together in a loose federation with the kings meeting each fifth and sixth year to sort out disputes by discussion and consensus. The laws they lived by were engraved on a pillar in the temple of Poseidon.

Although there were imports, the island as a whole was economically self-sufficient. Metals were mined extensively and cereal crops cultivated. Fruit farming was a widespread occupation with the fruit pressed for juice or oil – the latter product suggesting the possibility of olive groves, or something similar.

The Atlanteans constructed temples, palaces, docks and bridges. Among their more impressive engineering works was a canal 295 feet wide, 100 feet deep and '50 *stadia*' long. A Greek *stadium* varied in length locally from 505 to 705 feet and while we can't know for sure which measure Plato was using, the minimum length of the Atlantean canal must have been 4.8 miles.

The ringed moats around the central island were supposed to have been built by the god Poseidon, which may be another way of saying they occurred naturally. But Atlantean engineers linked them with channels deep enough and wide enough to permit the passage of a trireme, a manoeuvrable Mediterranean warship about 120 feet long and 18 feet wide. Stone walls were built, then faced with bronze, and a now unknown (or possibly just untranslated) precious metal called *orichalcum*.

A temple to Poseidon, the ruling deity of Atlantis, was a *stadium* long, 328 feet wide and proportionately high. Its exterior walls were plated in silver with various reliefs highlighted in gold. There were a great many sophisticated artworks – Plato writes of a massive gold statue in a chariot drawn by six winged horses, surrounded by representations of 100 Nereids (sea-living goddesses) riding on dolphins. Around the temple there were also lifelike statues of the Atlantean kings and other personages of importance.

The central plain also showed signs of the Atlantean love of monumental engineering. It was surrounded by an artificial ditch 100 feet deep, a full *stadium* wide and, since it surrounded the entire plain, 10,000 *stadia* long. (Plato himself balked at these figures, but claimed to report them exactly as they had been given to him by Solon.)

Apart from its engineering prowess, the culture of the Atlanteans was advanced by any measure. Plato's account indicates they had domesticated the horse – there was a large public arena built for racing – and invented the chariot. They seem to have had metal weapons, an inference drawn from the fact that such weapons were specifically banned for the ritual slaughter of bulls. Writing had been developed, although Plato gives no indication of how far literacy extended into the general population. Wine-making was known and practised, as was the weaving of cloth and the use of dyes. Farming techniques were sophisticated. The island supported two harvests a year, one in winter watered by reliable rainfall, one in summer using extensive irrigation. The art of navigation was well developed: Atlantis was a maritime culture with a standing navy of some 1,200 ships.

It is difficult to know where to start in comparing this romantic picture with prehistoric reality as propounded by the orthodox consensus.

First of all, the concept of a political federation is far too sophisticated for the world as it was more than 11,000 years ago. What you had at the time were scattered communities whose life was dominated by food gathering and hunting. Even the idea of a king, in the sense it was known to the Greeks of Plato's day, is far too advanced for the era. There may have been tribal chieftains, but not the formal division of territory under a single leader that Plato describes.

Equally out of order is the notion that the Atlanteans cultivated cereal crops and orchards. As we've already seen, agriculture was not developed anywhere on Earth before the ending of the Ice Age. And remembering the Ice Age, which was, of course, unknown to Plato, helps us demolish the fantasy of a two-harvest year, even if we were to allow the equally outlandish notion that the Atlanteans knew about irrigation. The weather would simply have been too cold.

Next comes the question of mining and metalworking. According to Plato, the Atlanteans worked gold and silver and used some other (harder, less precious) metal for weaponry. Bronze, an alloy of copper and tin, is specifically mentioned as a plating for walls. The modern term 'Bronze Age' describes a cultural development, not a specific time, but we know well enough when bronze was first used in various parts of the world. In Britain, for example, it did not appear until about 1900 BC. The Mediterranean peoples, possibly a better comparison with any supposed Atlantean civilisation, began using it just over 1,000 years earlier. Nobody, but nobody, was using bronze in 9600 BC.

Nobody was fermenting grapes for wine, or riding horses either. Although the primitive peoples of the day may possibly have painted their faces and certainly painted some caves, there is no indication they used dyes to colour their clothes, which, in any case, would have consisted of furs and skins.

Against this background, Plato's exaggerated claims about Atlantean skills in monumental engineering fall into stark perspective. So does the idea of Atlantis as a far-flung maritime empire with colonies in Europe, Africa and the Americas. At that time, nobody had the navigational skills to sail the Mediterranean, let alone the broad Atlantic. Nobody had the ships. Atlantean triremes were obviously a fiction derived from the state of Greek shipping in Plato's own day, as fanciful as the claims of some dotty modern writers that the Atlanteans once used aircraft and laser ray-guns.

There is scarcely a word of Plato's long description of Atlantis and its culture that could possibly be true. Or is there?

3

AMERICAN EVIDENCE

_____ **FACT** _____

PLATO'S CLAIMS OF ADVANCED ENGINEERING SKILLS
IN THE DISTANT PAST WERE ACCURATE.

The Aztecs were a Nahuatl-speaking people who ruled a large empire in what is now central and southern Mexico during the fifteenth and early sixteenth centuries AD. They were astonishingly sophisticated for an aboriginal people. By contrast with the native North American nations who lived in tepees, wigwams and other portable lodges, the Aztecs built cities, paved roads and ruled an expansive and expanding empire.

The Aztec capital, Tenochtitlan, covered 3 square miles and housed 300,000 citizens. Peter Tompkins describes it as 'glimmering like an exotic Venice at the end of a wide causeway, with stunning palaces, temples and pyramids, stuccoed pink with volcanic ash, rising from the cerulean waters of the lake'.[5] The lake was the Lake of the Moon, where the Aztecs founded their capital in 1325.

_____

[5] In *Mysteries of the Mexican Pyramids*, Thames & Hudson, London, 1987.

The city was a remarkable feat of civil engineering. The Aztecs first excavated mud from the bed of the shallow lake to make a series of artificial islands which they then turned into exotic and extensive kitchen gardens. Their great city itself was raised on a central island, and causeways and bridges were built to connect it to the mainland. Aqueducts were installed to ensure a plentiful supply of clean water. A vast public transportation system was created by digging a series of interlinked canals. Tompkins's analogy with Venice is apt. Tenochtitlan compared favourably in architecture and beauty with any Old World city of its day. The city skyline was dominated by limestone-faced stepped pyramids topped by stone-built temples.

It was a carefully planned city, like modern-day New York or Washington. There were four distinct quarters, each consisting of five further subdivisions, but the entire city was split by two rigorous class distinctions. The king and nobility lived in the area of the Great Temple. The rest was left to merchants and artisans.

Spanish records show Tenochtitlan housed no fewer than 500 stone-built palaces, crowned with battlements and ornamented with serpents. There were forty towering mansions within the courtyard of the Great Temple which were used as homes for the aristocracy. Trade flourished. A busy market brought in some 60,000 people every day. Tribute flowed in from conquered territories and there was a thriving export trade throughout Central America.

The Aztecs were not only exceptional engineers, but seem to have been capable mathematicians and astronomers as well. They had a definite taste for the monumental. One of their circular calendar stones is currently on display in the National Museum of Anthropology in Mexico City. It measures 12 feet in diameter and weighs more than 25 tons.

The Aztec Empire was still vigorous when the Spanish Conquistadors arrived in 1519 and halted its expansion for ever. Their origins are obscure. Consensus has it that they migrated

south from northern Mexico in the fourteenth century, and orthodox historians insist they originated there, despite the fact there
are no archaeological signs of their cultural development anywhere
in Central America. The Aztecs themselves told a different story.
They said they hailed from Aztlan, a land to the east. Given Plato's
claim that Atlantis established colonies on the continent beyond
the Atlantic Ocean, this is a curious coincidence. But it is not the
only coincidence to be found in South America.

When the Aztecs reached Mexico in 1325, they must have
noticed, near the site of their new capital, a round, stepped pyramid which, even then, would have displayed signs of great age.
It was constructed of cyclopean stonework, laid without mortar,
and approached by enormous elevated causeways. Today, we have
no idea who built the Pyramid of Cuicuilco, as it is now known.
It was excavated in 1920 by a team led by the American archaeologist Byron S. Cummins, funded by the National Geographic
Society in Washington and approved by the Mexican government
which seconded to the project two its ablest men, Dr Manuel
Gamio and Jose Ortiz of the Anthropology Office.

Cuicuilco is located fairly close to Mount Xitli, a volcano that
erupted at various times in the past to send lava flows rumbling
around three sides of the pyramid to cover an area of some 60
square miles. The lava hardened into a layer of volcanic rock
which today bears the name of the Pedrigal.

When Cummins carried out his excavation, he discovered the
base of the pyramid was buried beneath 15 to 20 feet of accumulated debris, which in turn had been covered by three separate
lava flows rising in places to a further 20 feet. Oddly enough, the
molten lava had not damaged the structure – and for a very
curious reason. Even at the time of the first Xitli eruption, the

pyramid had been buried in rock, soil, ash and pumice to such a degree that the lava never actually touched it. On top of the lava, now solidified to become the Pedrigal, a further 3 feet of soil had formed. Given this unusual geological picture, it was clear that the pyramid itself must have been of immense age. Cummins set out to put a figure on it. He took careful measurements of accumulations, relating them to the dating of known Xitli eruptions. When he finished his calculations he had a date not for the building of Cuicuilco, but for the time when it was finally abandoned and left to fall in ruins. That date showed Cuicuilco was already an ancient monument 8,500 years ago.

The city of Tiahuanaco is situated near the southern shore of Lake Titicaca, in Bolivia. Even in ruins it is an impressive site. Its principal structures include a huge stepped pyramid of earth faced with cut andesite (the Akapana Pyramid) and a rectangular enclosure known as the Kalasasaya, constructed of alternating stone columns and rectangular blocks. The entrance to the Kalasasaya is a monolithic gateway decorated with carved figures.

Tiahuanaco is an example of engineering so monumental that it dwarfs even the work of the Aztecs. Stone blocks on the site weigh anything up to 65 tons. They bear no chisel marks, so the means by which they were shaped remains a mystery. The stone itself came from two different quarries. One supplied sandstone and was situated 10 miles away. It shows signs of having produced blocks weighing up to 400 tons. The other supplied andesite and was located 50 miles away, raising the question of how the enormous blocks were transported in an age before the horse was domesticated in South America.

Close examination of the structures shows an unusual technique behind their building. The stone blocks were notched, then fitted together so that they interlocked in three dimensions. The result was buildings strong enough to withstand earthquakes.

Until very recently, orthodox archaeologists labelled Tiahuanaco a ritual site. The reason was that it was built as a port. It has docks, it has quays, it has harbours. But they are docks, quays and harbours that can't be used by any ship. Tiahuanaco is situated 13,000 feet above sea level and is miles from the nearest water. Faced with this mystery, the historians solved it by deciding Tiahuanaco was never lived in. It was, rather, a massive monument to ancient gods, built as a port, presumably, so souls could sail to heaven.[6] This idea, like the Tiahuanaco harbours, no longer holds water. By 1995, new archaeological discoveries clearly showed it was once not only a bustling metropolis, but also the capital of an ancient empire extending across large portions of eastern and southern Bolivia, north-western Argentina, northern Chile and southern Peru.

One of its most extraordinary accomplishments was a unique system of agriculture that involved the creation of raised planting surfaces separated by small irrigation ditches. These ditches absorbed sunlight and prevented crops from freezing, even on the high Altiplano. Algae collected from the ditches was used as fertiliser. The discovery of this ancient system has proven a godsend for modern Bolivian farmers who have found it gives greatly increased yields over modern methods.

The excitement of the recent archaeological finds has diverted attention from the original mystery – why would the Tiahuanacans build a working port 13,000 feet above sea level? One answer may be that they didn't.

There is considerable controversy about the age of Tiahuanaco. Some scholars argue that building started around 150 BC and the

---

[6] Much the same decision was taken when excavations revealed boat pits beside the Great Pyramid in Egypt.

city continued to grow until the latter part of the first millennium AD. Others insist it's much older and was probably in place
by the second millennium BC. Firmly in the latter camp are
Arthur Posnansky, an archaeologist whose findings were endorsed
by the Bolivian government, and Rolf Müller, a German astronomer with an interest in the site. Posnansky was the first to
suggest the Kalasasaya enclosure functioned as an astronomical
observatory, a thesis that is now widely accepted by his peers. But
Posnansky also used this insight to date the complex and came
up with the astonishing figure of 15,000 BC. Dr Müller checked
his calculations and cautioned that while 15,000 BC was certainly
a possibility, the astronomical findings could also point to
9300 BC.

Although both these dates have proven too much for the
archaeological consensus to swallow, they would certainly solve
the puzzle of why Tiahuanaco was built as a port. There is clear
evidence that the Altiplano on which the city is built only rose
above sea level with the ending of the Ice Age, around 8000 BC.
If Tiahuanaco existed before then, it would have functioned as a
port.

But if Tiahuanaco existed before then, it would have been a
sophisticated maritime city, more or less contemporary with
Plato's lost Atlantis.

According to the orthodox archaeological consensus – the same
consensus that insists Atlantis was impossible – the Americas were
first populated by migrants from Asia. They arrived sometime
prior to 8000 BC, the time the Ice Age ended and sea levels rose
to flood a land link that once bridged the Bering Strait between
Alaska and Siberia.

The wave – or waves – of migrants colonised what is now

Canada and gradually pushed south. With no Panama Canal to impede their progress, they eventually moved into the southern continent and there spread until they reached Cape Horn. Experts think the main migration took place around 12,000 BC. Two broad early cultures became evident. The first of these was the Paleo-Indians of the Great Plains and eastern North America. They seem to have become established sometime between 9000 BC and 11,000 BC, and were essentially Stone Age hunters who slaughtered mammoth until it became extinct, then moved on to buffalo. It's a curious fact that this culture shows a pattern of weaponry decline. Chipped-stone points made around the end of the Ice Age in 8000 BC were noticeably more crude than those dating 1,000 years earlier.

The second of the early cultures was an adaptation of food-collecting peoples to the inhospitable desert ranges of the western North America basin. These desert-dwellers were established by about 9000 BC, lived in caves and showed great ingenuity in the use of anything they found. They produced snares, twine, nets, baskets and even sandals from vegetable fibres. Millstones were created to grind wild seeds and flint was pressed into service to make tools and weapons.

It was the people of the Desert Culture who first discovered agriculture. At their currently known southern limit in Mexico, archaeologists have found indications that native American squash, peppers, and perhaps beans, were cultivated as early as 6500 BC. By about 3600 BC a primitive variety of corn (maize) first appeared in the Puebla area of south central Mexico.

The transition from agriculture to urban civilisation was slower in the Americas than it was in the ancient Near East. Urban centres only began to spring up between 2000 and 1500 BC in Meso-America and Peru, and hardly at all in North America until the arrival of Europeans. There were two exceptions to this general rule in North America. One was the village-based Hopewell culture that arose in Illinois and Ohio around 400 BC and produced some spectacular earthworks. The other was the Mississippi culture that arose, as its name implies, in the Mississippi Valley around AD 800, and was characterised by small towns which survived until the arrival of Europeans in the early sixteenth century.

Oddly enough, the overall picture of migration, which places the first inhabitants in the far north, is contradicted by the evidence. The earliest remains so far discovered are dated around 18,000 BC and were found in central Mexico. Orthodox historians blame the discrepancy on the ending of the Ice Age. They say the subsequent flooding must have hidden the more northerly signs of occupancy.

Despite this small hiccup, the archaeologists hold firm to their belief that the Americas reflect the same sort of linear progression as the Old World. The business of the Aztec homeland is sheer coincidence. Tiahuanaco is nowhere near as old as the astronomers have claimed. There is absolutely nothing in the archaeological record to suggest the influence of some mythical Atlantis. Except possibly the earthworks.

In July 1892, surveyors working to establish the boundary line between the United States and Mexico discovered a gigantic earthwork dam in Animas Valley, New Mexico. It stretched for nearly 6 miles and would, when functional, have enclosed a reservoir some 5 miles long and 0.25 miles wide, holding water to a depth of 20 feet. An estimated 8 to 10 million cubic yards of material had been moved to create the structure. The survey engineers reported what appeared to be traces of two further enormous dams within about 8 miles of this one.

Who built these structures? The plain fact is nobody knows. But they are not the only indications that engineers, accustomed to gigantic projects, were at work in the Americas in deep pre-history. Ancient irrigation canals at Pueblo Grande, Arizona, were first discovered in 1697 and have attracted intermittent attention from archaeologists up to the present day. Two of these canals were enormous – 85 and 60 feet wide from crest to crest – and extended for at least 7 miles in the case of one canal, and 9 miles in the case of the other. It is impossible to date these structures accurately since they have never been fully excavated.

The Americas are littered with ancient engineering works of a scale similar to those Plato attributed to the Atlanteans. Stone-wall fortifications, using blocks weighing up to one ton, run through the Berkley and Oakland Hills. Monk's Mound near Cahokia, Illinois, is 1,000 feet long, more than 700 feet wide, and is still 100 feet high. There is a stone fort with walls 8 feet thick near Massie's Creek in Ohio. The building work is super-ficially crude, but at the gateways the stones have been subjected to such intense heat that they have fused together.

In 1931, Matthew W. Sterling, head of the Bureau of American Ethnology, discovered a well-planned and fully integrated series of earthworks covering an area 1 mile square in the Florida Everglades near Lake Okechobee. The site includes a platform 30 feet high and 250 feet long, and the structures are laid out with mathematical precision.

Aerial photography in 1931 revealed the ruins of the Great Wall of Peru, a mind-bending stone structure that varied from 12 to 15 feet in width, was up to 15 feet high and ran for more than 50 miles. There were fourteen forts along its length, some covering an area of 200 feet by 300 feet with stone walls 15 feet high and 5 feet thick.

None of these amazing structures proves the Atlanteans estab-lished colonies in the Americas. But they do show that Plato's claims of advanced engineering skills in the distant past were accurate.

4

MYSTERIES IN EGYPT

——————— FACT ———————

... THERE WAS CIVILISATION IN EGYPT FAR EARLIER

THAN WE HAVE PREVIOUSLY SUPPOSED.

The Americas are not the only area of the world to provide examples of construction on a monumental scale.

There is a cut stone block in the Lebanon so immense (it weighs an estimated 1,000 tons) that it lies beyond the capacity of the world's largest crane to lift. At some point in prehistory, our ancestors were prepared to drag it halfway up a mountain.

Newgrange, in Ireland, a structure older than the pyramids, consists of an enormous artificial mound, a stone-lined inner chamber and a surrounding circle of megaliths, each weighing many tons. It represents an extraordinary feat of engineering, yet Newgrange is only one of three similar giant mounds and many other lesser megalithic structures that make up what archaeologists call the Boyne Valley Complex.

The massive megaliths on Malta, in Britain, in France and many other countries stand today as tokens of an engineering tradition that stretches back into the depths of prehistory. It was a tradition inherited by our earliest civilisations, nowhere seen more clearly than in Egypt. Monumental temple buildings survive as testimonials to Egyptian expertise in working stone. Although some were raised in sandstone, many more were built using incomparably harder granite, which is far more difficult to work. Granite was also used extensively for obelisks, with which so many pharaohs commemorated their reigns. These giant fingers pointing at the sky reach heights of up to 101 feet and can weigh hundreds of tons. An unfinished one in the quarries at Aswan has an estimated weight of more than 1,000 tons.

We know, more or less, how obelisks were cut from the granite bedrock, but we have no idea at all how they were moved – the unfinished giant obelisk at Aswan would have been beyond any construction machinery in use today. Once moved, as moved they were, we can only guess how they were erected. A British television production crew recently attempted to match the erection of the smallest known obelisk using only manpower – widely believed to have been the only thing available to Egyptian engineers. Despite the input of experts and considerable ingenuity in equipment, the attempt failed.

As has often been pointed out, the means by which the Old Kingdom Egyptians raised their immense pyramids at Giza remains a total mystery . . . except to those Egyptologists who cling to the myth that earthen ramps were used. The British master builder, Peter Hodges, has shown that an earth ramp would not do, because of the problem of retaining the sides.[7] He dismisses the suggestion of mud-brick ramps on the grounds that this material would crumble under the loads it would have to bear. If a ramp was used at all, the necessary stability could only have been achieved using squared stone. But whether made from earth, brick or stone, the volume of practical ramps would be three times that of the pyramids themselves and their length

[7] In *How the Pyramids Were Built*, Element Books, Shaftesbury, 1989.

would be approximately one mile, taking them off the Giza plateau and well into the desert.

Faced with this objection, archaeologists determined to cling to orthodox theory have suggested spiral ramps, but disposal of ramps of whatever design presents a problem. Spreading the constituent material of just one of them to a depth of 6 feet would cover a 700 acre area. Architect Julian Keeable has calculated that the combined volume of material needed for ramps servicing the three main pyramids would be an absolute minimum of 5 million cubic feet and, given a realistic ramp gradient, could approach five times that figure.[8] There is no indication of this amount of waste material having been disposed of in the vicinity of the Giza plateau.

Ancient Egypt, so far as we are aware, was without the wheel and consequently without the pulley, which relies on wheel technology. Without ramps how did they get the massive blocks – ranging in weight from 2.5 to 50 tons – up there? Hodges believes they used levers, and has conducted experiments to show that lever power can lift far heavier loads than most of us would imagine. Interestingly, the Greek historian Herodotus records an ancient tradition that levers were used. But even granting the stones were moved by levers, Hodges does not explain how they were set in place with optical precision. Nor will the use of levers explain how the Great Pyramid, the largest of the three main structures at Giza, was aligned precisely to the cardinal points, or how it came to incorporate the value *pi*.

These small mysteries are compounded by the fact that the Great Pyramid appears to be a stylised, but mathematically accurate, representation of the northern hemisphere. Claims to this effect were made centuries ago by classical authors, dismissed by Egyptologists, but confirmed by fresh measurements made in 1925. More recently, several authors have noticed that one line

---

[8] *Ibid.*

passing through the pyramid divides the planetary landmass into two near equal halves, while another provides near equal hemispheres of land and water.

The multiplying mysteries of the Great Pyramid have been treated so extensively elsewhere that it would be superfluous to present an exhaustive listing here.[9] Besides which, the pyramids are not, surprisingly, the most impressive examples of ancient Egypt's engineering skills: merely the best known.

Abydos, located in the low desert, west of the Nile, near al-Balyana some 90 miles north of Luxor, is one of the most important archaeological sites in Egypt. The ancient city was a royal necropolis and later a pilgrimage centre for the worship of Osiris. Excavations at the end of the nineteenth century by Emile-Clément Amélineau and Flinders Petrie uncovered a series of pit tombs belonging to the kings of the first two dynasties of Egypt. They also discovered impressive brick funerary enclosures at the north-western end of the necropolis. One was so extensive it covered nearly 2 acres. Today, tours to this site tend to concentrate on the beautiful New Kingdom Temple of Osiris, built by Seti I, but the real mystery of Abydos is centred on what is now called the Oseirion.

Visits to the Oseirion are sometimes discouraged because portions of it are now under water, the result of a major rise in the water-table since the foundations were laid. Even so, it's possible

[9] See, for example, Peter Tompkins's *Secrets of the Great Pyramid*, Allen Lane, London, 1973; or, more recently, *The Orion Mystery* by Robert Bauval and Adrian Gilbert, Heinemann, London, 1994; *Keeper of Genesis* by Robert Bauval and Graham Hancock, Heinemann, London, 1996; *Fingerprints of the Gods* by Graham Hancock, Heinemann, London, 1995; or my own *Martian Genesis*, Piatkus, London, 1998.

to appreciate the impact this curious structure had on the archaeologists who rediscovered it in the early years of the twentieth century.

In the *Annual Report of the Smithsonian Institution* for 1914, Edouard Naville concluded that the current excavations had unearthed the well of Abydos described by the Greek geographer/historian Strabo, in Book XVII of his *Geographical Sketches*. According to Strabo, the well was to be found near the Seti temple, but was itself subterranean and remarkable for the enormity of the stone blocks which formed the ceiling of its corridors. What may be seen today is impressive enough. The architecture is wholly unlike that of the Temple of Osiris – or any other New Kingdom temple for that matter. If anything, it is reminiscent of the ancient Valley Temple of Chephren, at Giza. Massive pillars of red granite weighing up to 100 tons each can be seen as you move towards the chamber traditionally believed to be the Tomb of Osiris. Close to this 'tomb' Naville and his team discovered a vast subterranean reservoir. He describes it in his Smithsonian article:

> Nothing revealed its presence; the entrance to it was exactly like that of all the other cells, the back of it being walled up after they had dug . . . it. The discovery of this subterranean reservoir, constructed of huge building stones, presents many questions. . . . We could not get to the bottom . . . as it is obstructed by a number of large blocks thrown there at the time the edifice was destroyed.

The cyclopean nature of the stone slabs used to build the reservoir is highlighted by the fact that Naville talks of broken *fragments* weighing several tons. Making the inevitable comparison with the Giza temple, he has this to say:

> Up to the present time, what is called the temple of the Sphinx at Gizeh has always been considered one of the

most ancient edifices in Egypt. . . . The reservoir of Abydos being of similar composition, but of much larger materials, is of a still more archaic character. . . . The pyramids are perhaps of the same age, but a pyramid is simply a mass of stone and is not a complicated design like the reservoir.

If we have here the most ancient Egyptian structure . . . it is curious that it should be neither a temple nor a tomb, but a reservoir, a great hydraulic work. This shows that the ancients well understood the flow of subterranean waters, the laws which control their rise and fall.

The point is well made, particularly since the sheer size of the stones make the Abydos reservoir an engineering work difficult, if not impossible, to duplicate today. Even if, as most modern Egyptologists believe, the Oseirion and its associated reservoir were built by Seti I, it is a remarkable feat of engineering. If, as Naville conjectured, it is actually contemporary with the Giza pyramids, then we have a further indication of the astonishing ability of the Old Kingdom Egyptians to handle stones more massive than anything we would comfortably tackle now.

But there is a third possibility, which deepens the mystery still further. The iconoclastic John Anthony West, a persistent thorn in the side of orthodox Egyptology with his insistence that this civilisation is far more ancient than the scholars allow, has made an extraordinarily interesting observation at Abydos.[10]

West notes that what is now taken as the bedrock on which Seti built his temple is actually compressed silt from the Nile. Once this is realised, it seems reasonable to assume that the Oseirion was not originally the semi-subterranean structure it is today, but was built on level ground and subsequently buried by

[10] In his *Traveller's Key to Ancient Egypt*, Quest Books, Illinois, 1995.

the silting of Nile floods. But such high-level floods date back to 10,000 BC, which would give the Oseirion an antiquity of more than 12,000 years. The reservoir might be older still.

In the mastabas tombs of Saqqara, Egyptologists have unearthed another mystery. Among the artefacts discovered in these ancient burial chambers were several slim-necked jars. The jars are made from diorite, the hardest stone on earth. They consist of a long, thin, elegant neck topping off a bulbous body. The vessels, neck and body, have been hollowed out to leave a wafer-thin shell. The mystery is, how did the Egyptians make them?

The mastabas of Saqqara are among the oldest surviving structures of ancient Egypt. They are extensive, mud-brick ruins of what were once tombs of the earliest dynastic kings. They are older than the pyramids. According to the current scholarly consensus, they date no later than 2575 BC but could be as early as 3050 BC. This means that the slim-necked jars they housed are between 4,000 and 5,000 years old.

Today, there is no technique known that would enable us to duplicate those jars. Tempered steel will scarcely scratch a piece of diorite. But even if the earliest Egyptians had this metal — which all the experts insist they did not — we cannot imagine what sort of tool could be inserted into the slim neck of such a vessel in order to hollow out its inside.

Even apart from the mastaba jars, the way the Egyptians handled diorite is something of a mystery. An Old Kingdom statue of the pharaoh Kephren, in this dark-coloured Nubian stone, remains one of the world's finest artworks, almost photographic in its attention to detail. Yet Egyptologists insist the hardest chisels of the time were made from copper, a soft metal wholly incapable of working this stone.

The mystery of how diorite was worked is matched by the mystery of how the Egyptians worked granite. Thousands of visitors to the Great Pyramid at Giza have gazed in admiration at the chocolate-coloured granite sarcophagus in the King's Chamber, without realising it too is a mystery. The puzzle, first recognised by the father of Egyptology, the respected British archaeologist Flinders Petrie, is that to hollow the sarcophagus from its constituent granite would require the use of diamond-tipped drills at a pressure of 2 tons. We can achieve this today without too much difficulty, but only by means of power tools. We have no idea at all how the Egyptians managed it.

We have no idea how the Egyptians managed to coat copper vessels with a micro-thin layer of antimony either. At a later time, the plating of artworks and utensils was achieved by beating on thin sheets of metal – gold, silver or whatever. It was a crude process characterised by hammer marks and relatively thick plating. The antimony plating, found in the earliest Old Kingdom and pre-dynastic artefacts, is of a wholly different order.

In 1933, Dr Colin G. Fink, then head of the division of electro-chemistry at Columbia University, suggested the Egyptians must have known of electro-chemical exchange – electro-plating – a process thought to have been discovered in the nineteenth century.

Much of Egyptian culture seems to have been like that. The further back you go, the more sophisticated the techniques become – the exact reverse of what the theory of linear evolution predicts. The pattern shows clearly in the most famous of all Egyptian preoccupations, pyramid building. The earliest known pyramid is that of Djoser, at Saqqara, built according to some chronologies only about sixty years before the Great Pyramid at

Giza, which itself followed a veritable orgy of pyramid building attributed to the pharaoh Sneferu.[11] A look at the sizes of these early dynastic and Old Kingdom structures tells its own tale.

Djoser's pyramid has an estimated volume of 432,000 cubic yards. The pyramids attributed to Sneferu at Meidum and Dashur are respectively 834,824 and 1,616,811 cubic yards in size. In the Giza group, the Great Pyramid of Khufu achieved a volume of 3,376,350 cubic yards and that of Khafre 2,889,902 cubic yards. The third Giza pyramid, that of Menkaure, is much smaller at 307,384 cubic yards. An unfinished pyramid at Zawiyet el-Aryan, possibly begun by Nebka, has a base size comparable to that of Khafre at Giza and might have finally rivalled it in volume. But once you move forward in time from these gigantic structures, the decline becomes evident. Never thereafter was a single pyramid built to match even the volume of Djoser's work. Only the Middle Kingdom pyramid of Senwosret II at Dashur (377,054 cubic yards) comes close. Few of the later pyramids achieved a volume of 250,000 cubic yards. Most struggled to top 100,000 cubic yards.

Size is not, of course, everything, but sheer engineering excellence follows exactly the same pattern of decline. The really ancient pyramids of Egypt stand proud today attracting tourists by the million. Many of the more recent structures are little more than mounds of rubble. It is as if the Egyptians once knew the secrets of monumental engineering – and a few other things besides – then gradually forgot them. But where could the Egyptians have learned these secrets in the first place?

---

[11] There is continuing academic debate about Egyptian dates, exacerbated in recent years by a new breed of Egyptologist who insist that some Egyptian structures, notably the Great Sphinx at Giza, are older than previously believed by between 4,000 and 9,000 years.

The history of ancient Egypt is, to say the least, peculiar. Even the most orthodox Egyptologist admits that the culture seems to have sprung up fully formed in the Nile Valley somewhere around 3100 BC.

The Egyptians themselves didn't believe this. Plato reported that their priests claimed the foundation of their state dated about 1,000 years after the foundation of Athens – that's to say, somewhere around 8600 BC. Texts discovered in Egypt itself suggest an even more venerable lineage. The surviving records are embodied in a list of kings drawn up by a priest named Manetho, who lived between 347 and 285 BC, and the Turin Papyrus, a manuscript dated around 1400 BC.

The earlier of these sources lists the familiar dynastic pharaohs, but claims there were three distinct periods in what is now thought of as Egyptian prehistory. The first was a line of pre-dynastic kings who ruled for 13,420 years. The second was a line of 'Horus-kings' (the exact meaning of the term is obscure) extending for a further 23,200 years. The final period, according to the Turin Papyrus, was a time of demi-gods, but the papyrus is damaged so we don't know how long they ruled.

According to Manetho, the pre-dynastic pharaohs went back some 13,777 years. He gave a combined dating for the Horus-kings and demi-gods of a further 15,150 years. Thus, depending on which source you consult, the Egyptians placed the foundation of their culture somewhere between 9000 and 37,000 BC.

While modern Egyptologists name and date the familiar pre-dynastic and Old Kingdom pharaohs with the help of these two documents, they dismiss the earlier claims as fiction. In this they are supported by the archaeological evidence. Although signs of habitation in the Nile Valley stretch back to 18,000 BC, there is no sign whatsoever of an advanced civilisation prior to 3100 BC

. . . unless you believe what geologists have been saying about the Sphinx.

The current controversy about the dating of the Great Sphinx at Giza has received so much publicity that it does not warrant treatment in any great detail here.[12] But the bottom line is relatively straightforward. An American professor of geology, Robert Schoch, was asked to estimate the age of the Sphinx – thought by Egyptologists to date from the Old Kingdom – on the basis of its pattern of weathering. Schoch, and other geologists who examined the stonework, concluded the weathering was caused by rainfall and not sand abrasion as had been previously assumed. On this basis, Schoch confidently dated the Sphinx somewhere between 7000 and 5000 BC. Some other experts believe it could be anything up to 5,000 years older.

These findings remain controversial, although rather more so among Egyptologists than geologists. But along with the advanced architectural, engineering and various other technical skills so unexpectedly evident in pre-dynastic and Old Kingdom times, they support Plato's contention that there was civilisation in Egypt far earlier than we have previously supposed.

---

[12] Interested readers will find a fuller account in my *Martian Genesis*, Piatkus Books, London, 1998.

5
ASTOUNDING
DISCOVERIES

——————————— F A C T ———————————

THERE REALLY *WERE* ICE AGE PEOPLES WHO CREATED

VAST ENGINEERING WORKS AND BUILT GREAT CITIES . . .

There seems to have been early civilisation elsewhere as well. According to the Old Testament, the Lord promised the Hebrew warrior Joshua that he would capture the city of Jericho if he was prepared to try a rather unusual military strategy. He was to surround the city with his army and walk around it once a day for six days. On the seventh day, he was required to make the march seven times preceded by seven priests bearing the Ark of the Covenant and carrying seven rams' horn trumpets. The Lord's final instruction was: 'And the priests shall blow with the trumpets. And it shall come to pass, that when they make a long blast with the ram's horn . . . all the people shall shout with a great shout; and the wall of the city shall fall down flat.' Joshua did as instructed and the walls came tumbling down.

Just how great a miracle this was only really came to light in 1952, when a team of British archaeologists, led by Kathleen Kenyon, began to excavate the Dead Sea site where Jericho once stood. What they found was, in Kenyon's own words, 'amazing'.

Although Joshua's army approached the city in 1425 BC, Jericho had existed long before then. Mesolithic traces were found, and carbon dated to somewhere around 9000 BC – only 600 years later than Plato's supposedly mythical Atlantis. There was definite proof of an organised community living in the city by about 8000 BC. By then, if not before, massive stone-built walls, 13 feet thick and 10 feet high, surrounded a 10-acre enclosure. At the centre stood an engineering masterpiece – a well-built stone tower with its own internal spiral staircase . . . *30 feet of which was still standing after nearly 10,000 years.*

But the sophistication of Jericho went beyond its famous fortifications. Kenyon unearthed extraordinary portrait sculptures created by the innovative technique of modelling plaster over human skulls to produce eerily lifelike results.

Nineveh, a city so old it is mentioned in Genesis, was situated on the east bank of the Tigris, opposite modern Mosul, in Iraq. It grew into the largest population centre of the ancient Assyrian Empire. Although not quite prepared to accept that it dates almost to the creation of the world, modern archaeologists believe it was founded no later than the seventh millennium BC. By Assyrian times, the boundary wall was more than 7 miles long and in places an almost unbelievable 148 feet thick. It had thirty great gates, several of them guarded by stone colossi.

In 1820, the brilliant Orientalist Claudius J. Rich became the first person in modern times to survey Nineveh. It was later excavated by French archaeologists, and in 1846 and 1847 by the distinguished English archaeologist Henry Layard, who discovered the palace of Sennacherib. Layard took back to England an unrivalled collection of stone bas-reliefs, several bronzes and thousands of clay tablets inscribed in cuneiform script. But it was while working at Nimrud, the earlier capital of Assyria, that Layard made his most intriguing find – a curious crystal artefact.

It was a disc, not quite circular since it had 0.2 inches discrepancy between its longer and shorter diameters. One face of the disc was flat, but the other had been ground to make it convex, using some sort of precision tool. Although no longer in pristine condition, it showed the remains of twelve cavities which had once contained condensed gases or liquids.

At first, archaeologists concluded the disc must be an ornament of some sort, but then David Brewster became interested in the find. Brewster was an eminent Scottish physicist noted for his experimental work in optics and polarised light. Today he is best remembered as the inventor of the kaleidoscope and the man who first produced three-dimensional images using a modified stereoscope. Brewster examined the artefact and announced, in 1853, that it was a well-made optical lens. This find is not unique. Some seventy-five similar lenses of varying dates have subsequently been found at sites that range from central Turkey through Crete to Troy. Current orthodoxy has it they were all decorative furniture inlays.

3

What an optical lens was doing in ancient Nimrud was then – and remains today – beyond the understanding of orthodox archaeology. But then so does the ancient 8.8-ton slab of man-made glass discovered in 1956 at Beth She'arim, south-west of Galilee. Similar weights of glass have been manufactured in modern times, but only rarely and for very specialised purposes – like the lenses of giant telescopes.

When faced with a find of cogged stone discs up to 6.5 inches in diameter in the Santa Ana River Valley, Ventura County, California, archaeologists fell back on the time-honoured explanation of 'ritual artefacts'. In this case, as in many others, the phrase is an admission of defeat. The plain fact is that no one has the least idea what the discs, which are more than 8,000 years old, were actually used for.

Once you begin to pay attention to what Michael A. Cremo and Richard L. Thompson aptly call 'forbidden archaeology'[13] – finds that fail to fit the current paradigm and are consequently ignored, explained away or dismissed as fraud – a wholly new and unexpected picture of the ancient world beings to emerge:

▲ A workable pregnancy test is described on a Babylonian clay tablet. It involved the insertion of a herbally impregnated woollen tampon into the woman's vagina. When removed and treated with an alum solution, the tampon turned red if the woman was pregnant.

▲ The Maya of South America knew how to drill teeth and repair cavities with metal fillings.

▲ People were tailoring their own clothes as long ago as 20,000 BC. The implements they used have been found. Excavation of three burial sites at Sunghir, Russia, in 1964 showed the men interred there had worn hats, shirts, trousers and moccasins. Excavation of the prehistoric mound of Çatal Hüyük, in central Turkey, revealed linen textile fragments, apparently from a girl's skirt.

▲ People who lived at Spirit Cave in northern Thailand seem to have been growing domesticated beans, peas, gourds and water chestnuts around 9000 BC. In faraway Palestine at the same period, the Natufians are known to have used sickles, although it's admittedly difficult to decide whether they were actually planting grain or simply harvesting wild crops.

▲ Map-making has a history of at least 12,000 years. A map was found in 1966 engraved on a mammoth tusk discovered at Mezhirich, in the Ukraine. It was dated to 10,000 BC and showed a local river flanked by a row of houses.

▲ Pottery jars were in use by the same date. A fine example was discovered in the Ishigoya Cave, on Honshu, Japan. Other pots found on the island were 1,000 years older (11,000 BC).

▲ Cheese-making, yoghurt-making and wine fermentation were all known in the Stone Age, according to recent discoveries.[14]

▲ Larger than life-size fingerprints are carved on a Neolithic dolmen on the Ile de Gavr'inis, Brittany, France. Most of the carvings show fingertip patterns typical of those on modern police files. Two are partial representations of palm prints. An article in the *Chronique Medicale* suggests the carvings may have been used as the ultimate identification references of tribal chieftains.

▲ The earliest boomerang, a hunting weapon with very specific and unusual aerodynamic properties, is dated at 21,000 years of age. It was found not in Australia, but in Poland.

▲ Oil lamps were made 20,000 years ago. They may have been used to light surgical operations on the human brain carried

---

[14] See *Ancient Inventions* by Peter James and Nick Thorpe, Michael O'Mara Books, London, 1995.

out at much the same time. There is an ancient tradition of anaesthetics, such as controlled doses of mandrake, which rendered patients immobile and insensitive to pain.

▲ Incredibly, copper was mined before flint in Serbia. There are prehistoric copper mines on Lake Superior, in California, Arkansas, New Mexico, Missouri, Illinois, Indiana, Georgia, New Jersey and Ohio, where prehistoric iron smelting furnaces have also been found. Manganese was mined near Broken Hill in Zambia. Carbon dating of charcoal on the site indicates these mines were being worked 28,130 years ago.

▲ In 1987, Birmingham University archaeologists, Lawrence Barfield and Mike Hodder, concluded that a mound of fire-cracked stones, excavated beside a stream in the city, had been a prehistoric sauna. Other similar sites have since been identified throughout Britain.

▲ The horse was domesticated in Europe sometime before 15,000 BC. A cave wall drawing at La Marche, France, shows one clearly wearing a bridle. So does an engraving found at the Grotte de Marsoulas, and another from St Michel d'Arudy.

▲ Archaeologists excavating tumuli on New Caledonia and the Isle of Pines in the south-west Pacific, discovered more than 400 man-made cement cylinders, 40 to 75 inches in diameter and up to 100 inches long. These cylinders, the purpose of which is unknown, were speckled with silica and iron gravel. Carbon dating showed they could be as old as 13,000 years.

▲ There are paved prehistoric roads in Yucatan, New Zealand, Kenya and Malta. There is a water tank in Sri Lanka with a surface area equivalent to Lake Geneva. There are 170,000 miles of underground aqueducts, thousands of years old, in Iran.

In 1932, Captain G. E. H. Wilson wrote in *Man* of a forgotten civilisation in East Africa's Rift Valley. Signs of this civilisation stretched across what are now Tanganyika, Ethiopia, Uganda, Kenya and Northern Zimbabwe and included terracing, ancient canals, drainage systems, miles of roadways and an irrigation system that appears to have included the diversion of whole rivers.

In June 1940, Froelich G. Rainey and Magnus Marks began excavating a Neolithic site near Ipiutak in the Arctic Circle. By the time they uncovered the remains of some 600 houses, with indications that at least a further 200 remained to be excavated, they realised they had stumbled on a prehistoric metropolis. The city was laid out on a logical grid and stretched for more than a mile. Artefacts and craftwork discovered at the site were of 'elaborate and sophisticated carving and . . . beautiful workmanship'. The archaeologists were convinced their find could not represent any proto-Eskimo culture, and decided instead that the people who built this chilly city must have entered the area from elsewhere.

Prehistoric stone-built structures on the Pacific island of Ponape, and on several neighbouring islands, indicate the presence in ancient times of yet another unknown civilisation. Writing towards the end of the nineteenth century, Royal Geographical Society member F. W. Christian described them as follows:

A massive breakwater runs along the edge of the . . . sea. Out to sea lie other islands, where there are scattered remains of another ancient sea wall. The most remarkable . . . ruins are on the Islet Tanack. The water front is filled with a solid line of massive stone-work about 6 feet wide and 6 feet above the shallow water-way. Above this is a striking example of immensely solid cyclopean masonry – a great wall 20 feet high and 10 feet thick.

Christian goes on to tell of various enclosures walled to a height of 40 feet and a massive subterranean vault roofed with enormous slabs of basalt.

A group of more than 90 man-made islands around Ponape covers an area of approximately 11 square miles. The group is protected by a reef, but to the east where the reef is broken, the ancient builders constructed a massive breakwater which stretches south for 3 miles. The basalt used in much of this work was transported a distance of 30 miles. The artificial islands are raised on basalt platforms anywhere from 5 to 10 feet above water level, then topped by huge walls – in the case of Nan Tauach, 30 feet high and 10 feet thick. An article in the *American Antiquarian* described the constructions as being 'among the world's prehistoric wonders'.

In 1928, the *Geographical Review* published a report on the discovery of ancient ruins on the site of Kevkenes Dagh, Asia Minor. This great isolated city, built by an entirely unknown culture, was three times the size of Boghaz Koi, the ancient Hittite capital. High-walled fortifications, 13 feet thick, enclosed an area of 1.5 miles by 1 mile.

Also in the 1920s came reports of the remains of cities, temples and monuments hidden in the wooded valleys stretching along the coastline through Honduras up to Yucatan. The remains were described as superbly carved monoliths and stones of immense size covered with ornaments and glyphs reminiscent of Egyptian, Indian and even Chinese art. An anonymous writer in *Pan-American Magazine* suggested they might be remnants of Atlantis. You can see why.

Yonaguni is a small island south-west of Okinawa in the Japanese archipelago. In 1988, scuba divers led by Kihachiro Aratake discovered an enormous stone structure on the seabed off the coast of Yonaguni. The structure lay more than 75 feet below the surface. Investigation showed it was 600 feet long, 450 feet wide and 90 feet high. The locals decided it was a natural formation.

Ten years later, the experts weren't so sure. The first geologist to investigate the site was Professor Masaki Kimura of Ryuku University on Okinawa. In April 1998, he discovered a structure divided into five distinct layers and decided it had to be man-made. It is easy to see why. Underwater photographs and video footage reveal a stepped, ziggurat-like monument of extraordinary proportions. Each step is about 3 feet high with clean edges and sharp angles. There is also an archway and two parallel monoliths among other intriguing features like drainage channels. Further investigation led to the discovery of smaller satellite ziggurats near the main edifice. Each is about 30 feet wide and 6 feet high. Each appears to be constructed of stepped slabs. Divers also found what looks like a road surrounding the main structure.

Robert Schoch, the American geologist who re-dated the sphinx, dived to examine the Yonaguni Monument and later commented that while natural water erosion and rock splitting might possibly produce a structure of this type, he had never seen anything quite like it before. Professor Kimura was even more forthcoming. He maintained bluntly that if the sharp steps were the result of natural erosion there would be debris on the seabed surrounding them. In fact there is none.

The aptly named Team Atlantis expedition who dived to make a video documentary of the site concluded that while the monument may be a natural formation in part, it had certainly been extensively modified by human hands. In other words, someone

in the depths of prehistory discovered a suitable rock formation
and used sophisticated engineering techniques to shape it the way
they wanted.

But if the various structures in the Yonaguni complex are
artificial, there is no known Japanese civilisation that could have
created them. Geological dating places the site above water no
later than 8000 BC. (The actual timespan is somewhere between
8000 and 10,000 BC.) Orthodox prehistory claims the most
advanced culture in Japan at the time was small groups of hunter-
gatherers. As Professor Kimura points out, there is no way they
could have built or even modified the Yonaguni Monument. He
believes for something of this size some sort of machinery must
have been involved.

America's William R. Corliss, a tireless collector of anomalies,
expresses the fundamental situation brilliantly:

> Most impressive of all . . . are the great deserted cities,
> the ruins of which stand on the lonely plains of Asia
> Minor, high in the thin air of the Andes, and on storm-
> swept Arctic shores. Here are signs of great civilisations
> that once prospered and raised magnificent walls, build-
> ings and monuments. Perhaps we have acclaimed the
> Greeks and Romans too loudly.[15]

Plato described Atlantis as a literate, seafaring culture which had
domesticated the horse, created vast engineering works and built

---

[15] Quoted from *Ancient Man: A Handbook of Puzzling Artifacts* by William R.
Corliss, The Sourcebook Project, Glen Arm, MD, 1980.

great cities. Its people wore clothes, mined and used metal, engaged in agriculture, drank wine and had some sort of centralised political structure. For anyone who subscribes to today's consensus of prehistory, this must all seem like an outlandish fantasy.

Yet, as we have now seen, there really *were* Ice Age peoples who created vast engineering works and built great cities, who wore clothes, mined and used metal, grew crops, drank wine and manifestly must have had some sort of centralised political structure. Even the question of literacy no longer seems quite so fantastic. Although the Sumerians are generally credited with inventing writing in the fourth millennium BC, a 1979 study by two American academics thinks otherwise.

Allan Forbes Jr and T. R. Crowder undertook an in-depth analysis of some curious signs which appear repeatedly in Upper Palaeolithic cave art. Unlike the rest of the art, these signs do not seem to be directly representational – that's to say they bear no obvious resemblance to any animal, person or artefact. Forbes and Crowder systematically considered, then eliminated, the possibility that the signs were meant to mark individual property, that they were hunting tallies or memory aids. The Americans then compared the signs with characters found in several early written scripts – Greek, Runic and Indus Valley signs – and found sufficient similarities to justify the belief that the later alphabets actually evolved from the prehistoric cave signs. They were left with only one conclusion, which they expressed forcefully in a paper published in *World Archaeology:* 'The sole remaining possibility is writing . . . a precursor form not differing fundamentally from inscriptions in early written languages.'

If we could just find evidence of maritime ability, it would almost seem as if Plato might one day be vindicated.

6

ANCIENT MARINERS

FACT

CHARTS DRAWN UP LONG BEFORE THE VOYAGES OF
COLUMBUS SHOW THE AMERICAS, AND BOTH THE
ARCTIC AND ANTARCTIC SEAS.

Pitcairn Island is an isolated, volcanic formation in the Pacific Ocean 1,350 miles south-east of Tahiti. It was named after the sailor who first sighted it in 1767, and is well known today because of the part it played in one of the most dramatic mutinies ever to take place aboard a British ship.

HMS *Bounty* was a 215-ton Royal Navy transport ship, assigned towards the end of the eighteenth century to a scheme for taking breadfruit trees from Tahiti to be replanted in the West Indies. The ship sailed to Tahiti under the command of William Bligh, a former shipmate of the famous explorer, Captain Cook. With its cargo of breadfruit trees, it was approaching the isle of Tonga on its return journey to Jamaica when, on 28 April 1789, it was seized by the Master's Mate, Fletcher Christian. Bligh was cast adrift in a longboat with eighteen crew members who had remained loyal to him.

Christian sailed the *Bounty* to Pitcairn where he, eight of his

fellow mutineers and a number of Tahitian men and women, dis-
embarked then burned the ship. They found the semi-tropical
island something of a paradise, and established their own colony
which went undiscovered until 1808.

The *Bounty* survivors, whose descendants make up the population of Pitcairn to this day, were not the first sailors to be ship-
wrecked on this Pacific speck. A rock inscription (which went
unreported until 1870 and has been roundly ignored ever since)
reads:

> Our crew, wrecked in a storm, made land, thank God.
> We are people from the Manu region. We worship Ra
> in accordance with the scripture. We behold the sun
> and give voice.

Manu is a highland area of Libya. The Pitcairn inscription is in
the Libyan dialect of ancient Egyptian.

In the early 1900s, a stone scarab – the premier ancient Egyptian
symbol of good luck – was dug up in a cane field at Hambledon,
Australia. In 1908, a farmer digging a hole for a fence post west
of Cairns unearthed an Egyptian coin dating from the reign of
Ptolemy X (107–88 BC). In 1969, Professor R. Gilroy, director
of the Mount York History Museum at Mount Victoria, went on
record, following the discovery of hieroglyphic carvings 50 miles
south of Sydney, with the opinion that ancient Egyptians may
have visited Australia.

Near the end of the nineteenth century, an article in the prestigious periodical *Science*, claimed that the ancient Egyptians had
developed a ship-railway across the Isthmus of Corinth. Apart
from the fact it used polished granite rails in place of metal, this

astonishing work of engineering was very similar to its modern counterparts. A similar railway may have been used to take ships overland across the Suez Isthmus.

According to the *Journal of the Polynesian Society*,[16] chin tattoos popular among the women of Upper Egypt at the turn of the twentieth century were identical to those favoured by Maori women in New Zealand. More curious still, the ornamental designs discovered on some of the oldest Egyptian mummies, are mirrored by the oldest traditional patterns of the Maori culture.

The Egyptians were not noted as mariners. Although there are a large number of ancient boat pits on the Giza plateau and two of them – excavated in 1954 – contained the remains of actual boats, most Egyptologists consider their use was purely symbolic. They believe the boats were to be used by the pharaoh after death for his journey to the afterlife, or the stars. The few dissenting voices who think the boats were real boats tend to assume they got no further than the Nile. To the experts, it would be preposterous to suggest the ancient Egyptians ever visited New Zealand. All the same, there's hard evidence the ancient Egyptians travelled a lot further than Egyptologists give them credit for.

3

The greatest maritime civilisation in the ancient Mediterranean was that of Minoan Crete, which began to develop, according to consensus chronology, around 2750 BC. It was, by any measure, an impressive culture.

When Arthur Evans excavated the Palace of Minos, at Knossos, in the early twentieth century, he discovered evidence of unbroken architectural and artistic development from Neolithic times. The palace itself rivalled anything ancient Egypt had to offer. It

---

[16] Issue 13, 1904.

was a quadrangular complex of rooms and corridors grouped around a great central court. Seaward, a great portico of twelve pilasters gave access to the central court and a rectangular open-air theatre spoke of sophisticated entertainments. An eastern wing originally rose four – perhaps five – storeys above the slope of the valley, while to the south-east, domestic apartments had running water and even flush toilets. A wide stairway led to an upper floor. The north-east part of the palace was devoted to offices and store-rooms. To the west was a series of storerooms containing great numbers of oil containers, many of them more than 5 feet tall. The state rooms yielded up a unique gypsum throne. Light was supplied from above by an ingenious system of wells, and colon-naded porticoes provided ventilation during hot Cretan summers. Both the interior and exterior of this great palace were decorated with brilliantly coloured frescoes.

By far the most sophisticated pottery of the time was made in Crete. Finely honed skills and refined techniques brought it to such a peak of perfection that containers were often thin as eggshells. It was work that was widely appreciated. Minoan pot-tery has been found throughout the Aegean and as far as Cyprus, Egypt and the Levant.

Trade made the culture wealthy. Goldsmiths produced work of exceptionally high aesthetic value. They were aware of and used techniques such as granulation and filigree. Gold sheets were cut and stamped into beads or other designs to make necklaces and diadems. Clothing was often decorated with gold. Minoan crafts-men became renowned for their work with gems.

Unlike almost any other empire of the time, the Minoan rulers built no fortifications. They had no need to. Their military strength, like their economic success, was firmly founded on con-trol of the sea lanes. Like Britain in the nineteenth century, it was sea power that kept the island safe – a policy that worked until about 1400 BC when an invasion from mainland Greece destroyed the culture. Until then, the Minoans were the undisputed masters of navigation in the Mediterranean, perhaps even in the entire world. An American historian thinks they owed their expertise to an even greater maritime civilisation that existed in the Ice Age.

Charles Hapgood is a professor at Keene State College, New Hampshire. His speciality is the history of science. One of his early books, *Earth's Shifting Crust*, carried an endorsement from Albert Einstein, who found it contained 'ideas of great importance to everything that is related to the history of the earth's surface'. Hapgood has also produced ideas of considerable importance to our understanding of prehistory. He believes, for example, that there existed in the remote depths of the last Ice Age, long before the appearance of the known historical cultures of Sumeria, Egypt, Greece and Rome, an ancient civilisation more advanced than any of them.

It was a civilisation that, if limited to a single location, had trade links across the globe – and might even have been a worldwide culture in the sense that the social and economic ideas developed largely in Britain and the United States now form the basis of a Westernised culture that is making inroads into virtually every region on the planet.

Hapgood has concluded that his Ice Age civilisation was probably more advanced – at least in some respects – than the great early cultures of ancient Egypt, Babylon, Greece and Rome. Indeed, he believes that in the specific areas of astronomy, navigation, mathematics, map-making and shipbuilding, it was more advanced than any country in the world earlier than the eighteenth century AD. He believes scientists of the prehistoric civilisation were capable of calculating the exact length of the solar year to a tolerance of two seconds . . . that its geographers had accurately measured the circumference of the Earth . . . that its mathematicians had a knowledge of spherical trigonometry . . . that its astronomers knew of the moons of Jupiter and the satellites of Saturn.

From the accomplishments of this civilisation, Hapgood has deduced an organised government and considerable economic resources. He is convinced it excelled in the arts of navigation to such a degree that it explored the Arctic and Antarctic seas, something not accomplished by our own culture until the nineteenth century. He is certain it had discovered a practical means of calculating longitude, something only achieved again in the 1700s.

Against the background of the current scientific paradigm in which the professor himself was educated, these are extraordinary beliefs. But Hapgood claims hard evidence. Every one of his conclusions is based on the careful analysis of ancient maps, themselves copies of originals whose structure indicates they were first drawn in the depths of prehistory. Hapgood speculates that while the charts originated with an unknown people, their knowledge was inherited by the Minoan sea kings of ancient Crete and the Phoenicians, who became for a thousand years the greatest sailors in the ancient world.

The prehistoric charts were possibly collected and studied in the great library at Alexandria, where compilations were extracted by the geographers who worked there. The library, which contained an estimated 1 million volumes and was reputed to embody the entire knowledge of the ancient world, fell foul of Julius Caesar whose attack on the city caused it to be burned to the ground. It was later restored and even enlarged, but in AD 391 was burned down by a Christian mob egged on by the patriarch Theophilus, and finally destroyed in the Arab conquest of Egypt 300 years later.

Although legend has it that the Arab destruction of the library was carried out because 'any wisdom not contained in the Koran was not worth keeping' the historical reality was that a body of ancient learning was preserved by Arab scholars throughout the

Dark Ages. Hapgood believes that the maps created in the Ice Age may have been transferred to Constantinople, a noted centre of learning, and carried off by the Venetians when they captured the city during the Fourth Crusade of AD 1204.

Most of the surviving charts which show prehistoric influence are of the Mediterranean and the Black Sea. But the more interesting and evidential take us further afield. Although drawn up long before the voyages of Columbus, these charts show the Americas, and both the Arctic and Antarctic seas. More astonishing still, the Antarctic continent is accurately mapped including contours which disappeared beneath an ice cap which is now more than a mile thick. We know the contours are accurate because of modern depth soundings. Hapgood simply assumes the ancient map-makers visited the continent before the ice cap formed.

With Hapgood's findings, almost all the elements of Plato's story are in place. Prehistorian Mary Settegast has presented evidence of many cultural and technological correspondences within the Straits of Gibraltar, including a great war in exactly the era Plato claimed.[17] Other equally respected archaeological sources have shown time and time again that the aspects of Plato's Atlantis, so long dismissed as mythic, are no more than the collecting together of prehistoric realities discovered elsewhere throughout the world.

There were massive engineering works carried out in the Ice Age. There were great cities built. Its peoples wore tailored clothing, drank wine, made cheese, inscribed written records, built ships and sailed the oceans to the farthest corners of the planet.

---

[17] In *Plato Prehistorian: 10,000 to 5000 B.C. Myth, Religion, Archaeology*, Lindisfarne Press, New York, 1990.

This is not to say, of course, that every part of the globe had achieved such cultural peaks, any more than every culture of the world today is based on computer technology. We still have our Bushmen and Aborigines pursuing an essentially Stone Age existence, and there are clear indications the same was true in prehistoric times. Yet as Hapgood himself puts it:

> The idea of the simple linear development of society from the culture of the . . . Old Stone Age through the successive stages of the . . . New Stone Age, Bronze and Iron Ages must be given up. . . . We shall now assume that, some 20,000 or more years ago, while Palaeolithic peoples held out in Europe, more advanced cultures existed elsewhere on earth.[18]

But suggestive though this weight of evidence may be, it still doesn't add up to Atlantis. Plato's throwaway mention of the twice-yearly Atlantean harvest is enough to give the lie to his fantasy. There could be no question of two harvests in an Ice Age. Unless, of course, our ideas about the Ice Age are all wrong, too.

---

[18] Quoted from *Maps of the Ancient Sea Kings*, by Charles H. Hapgood, Adventures Unlimited Press, Illinois, 1996.

7

PREHISTORIC PUZZLE

_____ **F A C T** _____

THE EVIDENCE INDICATES A WELL-FED, FIT AND

HEALTHY PEOPLE WHO HAD NO DIFFICULTY KEEPING

WARM DURING THE BIG FREEZE . . .

Science offers us a clear and detailed picture of the last Ice Age. It began 2.5 million years ago and ended (hopefully) about 8000 BC.[19] As you might imagine, it was a time of extreme cold. Almost a third of the planetary land surface (17 million square miles) was covered by vast sheets of ice. Huge stretches of the oceans froze.

The largest of the land-based ice sheets was the Laurentide, in North America. There were times when it grew to such monstrous proportions that it stretched all the way from southern Illinois right up to the Canadian Arctic. It was so broad it reached from the Rockies to Newfoundland. This was only one sheet. There were others. The Cordilleran formed in western Alaska and stretched to northern Washington. There were glaciers and ice

---

[19] Some scientists are not convinced it's over. They believe we are living in a brief inter-glacial and the ice will come again – perhaps even in our lifetime.

caps throughout the highlands of the western United States, Mexico, Central America, and Alaska. On the other side of the partly frozen Atlantic, the Scandinavian ice sheet at times covered most of Britain, central Germany, Poland and northern Russia to the Arctic Ocean. There were smaller ice caps in the highlands of northern Siberia and Arctic Eurasia. Glaciers formed in the Alps and elsewhere in the various European and Asian mountain ranges.

Although the northern hemisphere was worst hit, the southern hemisphere was not left unscathed. Ice caps and glaciers developed throughout the Andes. Glaciers formed in New Zealand, Africa and Tasmania. There were even great rivers of ice flowing from mountains standing on the equator.

In those areas of the world not actually covered by ice, conditions were generally grim. Temperatures were much lower than they are today. A 125-mile zone of permafrost clung to the southern border of the North American ice sheet. Europe and Russia fared even worse. Here, permafrost extended many hundreds of miles south. With the coming of the ice, temperatures plummeted. They remained around zero even at the southernmost reaches of the permafrost, while closer to the ice sheets they dropped to minus 6°C or lower. Air temperature was anything up to 20°C colder than it is today.

With so much water locked up in ice, sea levels fell dramatically. In 18,000 BP, for example, it is calculated that the drop was more than 300 feet. This gave rise to a world map somewhat different from what it is today. Every continent was larger. What are now submarine continental shelves were then exposed. There was a land bridge connecting Alaska with Siberia. The British Isles were part of mainland Europe. Even those areas far from the actual glaciers were influenced by their icy grip. With lowered sea levels and colder oceans, there were fewer tropical cyclones. The result was decreased rainfall. In a far-reaching domino effect, sand dunes became more active and arid zones increased in Australia,

Africa, India and the Near East. As glaciation peaked, the world's deserts expanded by a factor of five.

Despite the extreme brutality of the climate, life survived. Indeed, there is clear evidence that both plants and animals of the Ice Age were much the same as those living today, although they were differently distributed and included several species now extinct. According to the orthodox scientific scenario, it was during the Ice Age that humanity evolved.

The oldest example of our evolutionary line, *Homo habilis* ('Handy Man') appeared in Africa about 2 million years ago. *Habilis* (probably) evolved into *Homo erectus*, who spread out of Africa during the early Ice Age. Our own species *Homo sapiens*, appeared about 400,000 years ago.

It is easy to imagine how these people must have lived in the frozen northern hemisphere. They would have wrapped themselves in furs as a protection against the extreme cold, just as the old-style Eskimo lived under layers of caribou fur. But the analogy with the Eskimo is limited. At the height of the Ice Age there was little precipitation, hence there were extensive areas in which igloo building would have been impossible – for lack of snow – even if primitive humidity had stumbled on the technique. Nor could Ice Age humanity have constructed the driftwood cabins of the Eskimo. The first action of the ice sheets is to raze forests and ensure a scarcity of wood.

In summer, many Eskimo traditionally moved into animal-skin tents. Ice Age 'summers' were too chill to permit this without the aid of the oil-lamp heaters eventually adopted by the Eskimo – technology far too sophisticated for evolving humanity. Indeed, for most of the Ice Age, humanity had to survive without the most basic technology of all – the ability to make fire.

Against this background, it is logical to assume our fur-coated Ice Age ancestors huddled in the depths of caves and expended their short, brutal lives in a constant battle for survival. But logical or not, this picture is wrong.

Archaeological investigation has shown that 'cavemen' didn't live in caves. Most of our Ice Age ancestors made their homes beneath rock shelters, or in huts or tents. When they went near caves at all, it was to camp out in the cave mouth. This is peculiar. The deep interiors of natural caverns maintain a fairly constant temperature which, while still bitterly cold during an ice age, would be warmer than the murderous chill outside. It's easy to see why our ancestors would seek the shelter of a cave mouth. Why they didn't move more deeply in is harder to explain.

Two possibilities spring to mind. One is that they were afraid of predators, such as bear or lion, which themselves sometimes inhabited deep caves. The other is that they were afraid of spirits; that, in other words, they had a superstitious awe of the subterranean darkness.

The first of these possibilities is superficially appealing. We have become so accustomed to the myth of 'man the hunter' that we forget for most of our evolution, humanity was prey. But whether at the prey or hunter stage, humanity was never stupid. We would not have survived had we not learned to read the signs. It would have been simple enough to determine whether your proposed new home was already occupied. It would even have been possible for a determined human group to drive out the occupant. Besides, you are in just as much danger from bear if you camp in the mouth of a cave as you are if you make your home deep inside. Whatever the dangers, it would appear the people of the Ice Age could hold their own against the local predators. But were

they superstitious? Did unreasonable fear of spirits, so prevalent
in primitive communities, keep them out of the caverns? Here
again, the answer seems to be no. For while it is quite clear that
Ice Age humanity as a whole did not *live* in deep caves, there is
considerable evidence that such caves were often *visited*. A few –
a very few – show signs of brief stays. The reason they were visited is extraordinary: our ancestors decided to decorate their walls.

In 1876, when Don Marcelino de Sautuola raised a torch to examine the interior of a deep cavern on his Spanish estate at Altamira,
he discovered the first examples of prehistoric cave art to be seen
in modern times. But the art was so sophisticated in its execu-
tion, so technically advanced in style, that experts of his day were
universal in their condemnation of the whole find as a fake. Their
continuing attacks almost certainly contributed to de Sautuola's
early death in 1888.

The position of de Sautuola's critics was logical. The creation
of art requires sophistication and sensitivity. It also requires an
environment that can support leisure activity. It's difficult to see
how such an environment could have existed in the Ice Age.

Yet Ice Age art is not confined to a single site in Spain. There
were subsequent discoveries of artworks in Arabia, Australia,
Brazil, China, France, India, Japan, Korea, Kwazulu, Mexico,
Namibia, North America, Patagonia, Peru, Portugal, Sicily, Zaire
and Zimbabwe. Some are as old as 30,000 years, and may even
be 10,000 years older than that. There is even evidence for the
use of pigment dating back 125,000 years.

Such widespread distribution is utterly astonishing. Bear in
mind the global environment. The whole of Scandinavia lay
beneath a single ice sheet, like much of today's Arctic. Almost all
of northern Europe was devoid of woodland, chill wastes of

tundra broken only rarely in the most sheltered spots by a straggle of pinewood. The Baltic Sea was cut off from the North Sea and existed as little more than a deep, brackish lake. The Gulf Stream was diverted south. The area where London now stands was a open steppe.

It costs more energy to survive in a cold climate than a hot one. Archaeological excavation shows the prehistoric people of Europe lived on venison, fish and eggs. They were few in number. Tribal communities were small. Nature was unforgiving. If the hunting and the foraging were poor, they starved. In an Ice Age, every waking moment should have been devoted to the necessities of survival – the search for fuel, shelter, food and clothing. There should have been no time left over for frivolities like art.

Yet not only *was* there time left over, but skeletal remains show no sign of malnourishment. Despite the ice sheets and the permafrost, despite the perpetual cold, despite the harshest conditions our planet has ever known since the time of its creation, there is little indication of starvation or injury. There is no indication at all of illness. What the evidence indicates is a well-fed, fit and healthy people who had no difficulty keeping warm during the big freeze, and had sufficient leisure time to express their creativity in painting.

To date, about 275 decorated sites have been found in Europe alone, along with many more pieces of 'portable art' – statuettes, figurines, incised stones, and items of that sort. While the majority of these artworks are devoted to animal representations, a number show human figures. Almost without exception, the people appear to be lightly clad or naked.

Human figures in prehistoric art are generally far less well executed than animal paintings. Many are little more that matchstick people. But even matchstick people have a tale to tell. A scene painted in a shaft at the Lascaux caverns in France features, among other things, a man with an erection. There is no tenting or drapery of clothing around the prominent part, suggesting its owner was naked, at least from the waist down.

In the Los Casares cave, in the Spanish province of Guadalajara, is a depiction of a couple apparently preparing for intercourse. The man is dressed in a kilt open at the front. The women seems to be naked. Another couple, etched on a plaque recovered from excavations at Enlene, in France, are both naked.

It could, of course, be argued that our distant ancestors just found it convenient to undress for sex. But an ivory statuette from Hohlenstein-Stadel in Germany shows a standing figure in a tunic that leaves his arms and legs bare. Even more telling are the so-called 'Venus' figurines found across Europe. Typical of these females is the Venus of Lespugue, from the Haute Garonne region in France. This 5.7-inch-tall statuette shows a well-endowed woman wearing nothing but a loincloth.

Two stylised females engraved face to face on a plaque from Gönnersdorf in Switzerland are both obviously naked. 'Venus pebbles' from Kamikuroiwa in Japan are engraved with female torsos dressed in nothing more substantial than fringes over breasts and genitals. In one of them, the fringe – reminiscent of the Hawaiian grass skirt – is so sparse that the pubic triangle is visible.

The rock paintings of the Spanish Levant are exceptions to the rule that our ancestors concentrated on animal paintings. In rock shelters from the Pyrenees to the Sierra Nevada, human figures predominate. These artworks show women dancing, men hunting and warriors in battle. Archaeologist Mary Settegast describes their clothing:

> The head-dress . . . includes horns, animal masks and feathered headbands; numerous body ornaments and suggestions of body painting have been detected as well.

Fringed waistbands are common; animal skins are occasionally shown around the waist with tails hanging down; and while some of the warriors appear to be wearing 'knee-breeches' or loincloths, others wear nothing at all.[20]

The dating of these paintings is uncertain – one problem is that their style is unlike anything seen elsewhere – but a best-guess scenario places them no later than the beginning of the Middle Stone Age, and very possibly earlier. This means the figures were painted while the Ice Age still maintained its chilling grip.

The Levanzo cave on a small island off Sicily's western coast has a series of engravings which include a naked human grouping. The artwork has been dated between 8000 and 8500 BC.

Experts in the field routinely sex prehistoric rock art figures on the basis of whether or not they have visible breasts, vulvae or penises without stopping to ask why, in an era of hideous cold, any body part at all should be depicted as exposed. It is possible that cave paintings of humans were not supposed to be representational – even though depictions of animals certainly were.[21] Michelangelo's magnificent nudes on the Sistine Chapel ceiling are not, after all, an indication that sixteenth century Italians strolled about naked. But there is some evidence that the prehistoric artists were painting what they saw.

Prehistoric rock art is not limited to Europe, and in some areas there is a continuity of the tradition carried through to relatively modern times. Any study of the continuity clearly indicates that the art was meant to be representational – the artists depicted what was important to them, what most influenced their lives.

---

[20] In *Plato Prehistorian*, Lindisfarne Press, New York, 1990.

[21] So representational that it had to await the invention of the high-speed camera for us to realise the accuracy with which the prehistoric artists had depicted the legs of a galloping horse.

At Tassili N'Ajjer, in the Algerian Sahara, for example, there are scenes that include hunters and herdspeople, while paintings of charioteers and horses dating to 500 BC, may indice the influence of dynastic Egypt.

The nomadic San people of Tanzania, Zimbabwe, South Africa, and south-west Africa have a Pleistocene art tradition that has actually been carried through, uninterrupted, well into modern times. Among their more recent paintings are those which show European traders with stovepipe hats.

In view of this evidence, it is tempting to consider rock art as a sort of pictorial history of the tribe, a representation for posterity of life as it used to be, with highlights like the appearance of Victorian tradesmen faithfully recorded. But if this is so, humanity appears to have been under-dressed for an Ice Age.

There is a cave in Fontanet, France, which preserves fossil footprints of a child. These prints, along with a knee-print and hand-prints, are so numerous it is possible to deduce what the youngster was doing. She, or he, seems to have been chasing a puppy or young fox around the cave. There are similar footprints of both children and adults in caverns at Aldene, Tuc d'Audoubert and several other sites. All have one thing in common. They show the people of the Ice Age went around barefoot.

8

CRACKS IN THE CONSENSUS

———————— **FACT** ————————

COLD IN ITSELF DOES NOT LEAD TO GLACIATION. ONCE
YOU REALISE THIS, IT COMES AS (SLIGHTLY) LESS OF A
SURPRISE TO DISCOVER THAT THE FIRST PREREQUISITE OF
AN ICE AGE IS A RISE IN TEMPERATURE, NOT A FALL.

When geology emerged as a scientific discipline in the early nineteenth century, its pioneers were faced with widespread evidence that massive changes had affected the Earth in relatively recent times. Something had polished and scratched the surface of many rocks and the world was strewn with debris. There were literally millions of displaced boulders, known because of their location as 'erratics'. They appeared in the most peculiar places: delicately perched on mountain peaks, choking valleys in their thousands, or standing in splendid isolation in a meadow. The question that faced those early geologists was obvious: what had moved the boulders?

The mystery seemed somehow connected with the polished surfaces seen on some rocks and the striations seen on many others, including the erratics themselves. These striations had a common alignment – north-west to south-east – whether the rocks that bore them were found in the northern or southern hemisphere. Typically they appeared on the summits of high hills or on the northern or north-western slopes of mountains.

Clearly, whatever caused the scratches must have originated in the north or north-west and moved in a constant direction across the surface of our planet. It seemed logical to assume the same force that scratched the rocks had carried the erratics with it. But what was the nature of that force?

Whatever it was did more than carry boulders and scratch rocks. Gravel and sand deposits were found banked up against the northern or north-western slopes of mountains. Muggendorf, in Germany, was typical of many sites at which northward and north-westward facing caves and fissures were packed with these silts. Investigation indicated recent geological origins.

Early solutions to the problem were in keeping with their time. For centuries, the Western world had accepted the biblical story of a universal flood. Even scientists with an openly atheistic bent – rare enough at the beginning of the nineteenth century – were hard put to free themselves of the cultural influence. Almost without exception, early geologists concluded it was water that carried the erratics. They proposed terrifying scenarios of vast rivers overflowing, or gigantic submarine earthquakes creating enormous tidal waves.

In 1802, the first dissenting voice arose, John Playfair, a mathematician, concluded that glaciers were the only natural phenomenon capable of transporting rocks over large distances. He published his theory and was ignored.

Ice continued to hold a certain fascination. In 1821, a Swiss engineer named Ignaz Venetz published evidence of large-scale Alpine glaciation at some point in the past. The geologist Jens Esmarch soon afterwards proposed there had once been a much greater extension of the glaciers still seen in his native Norway. Just eleven years later, Professor A. Bernhardi was claiming that the (North) polar ice cap had formerly extended far south into Germany, thus explaining the extraordinary number of erratics on the German plain.

In 1837, glacial theory emerged again, this time in an even more spectacular form. The Swiss palaeontologist Louis Agassiz delivered a startling address to the Helvetian Society. In it, he proposed that erratics, till and striated rock pavements were all evidence of an Ice Age – a term he borrowed from the botanist and poet Karl Schimper, who had used it in one of his verses. Agassiz painted a vivid word picture of glacial ice extending from the North Pole to the shores of the Mediterranean. His ideas were not well received. Agassiz was best known for his work on fossil fish. One distinguished scientist, Alexander von Humboldt, advised him to get back to them. He ignored the advice and began intensive field studies. They confirmed his conclusions to such an extent that in 1840 he published his ground-breaking *Études sur les Glaciers* ('Studies of Glaciers') which demonstrated that Alpine glaciers had been far more extensive in the past. That same year he visited the British Isles to extend his glacial doctrine to Scotland, northern England and Ireland. In 1846 he travelled to North America where he found additional evidence for an Ice Age.

It was an idea whose time had come. Just two years later, Karl Ernst Adolf von Hoff, who was competing for a prize put up by the Royal Society of the Sciences in Gottingen, Germany, also denied the 'violent water' theory of erratics. He replaced it with the notion that drift ice might have carried the boulders and soon found his concept had attracted supporters.

Among them was Schimper, from whom Agassiz had borrowed the term *Ice Age* in the first place. Like von Hoff, Schimper believed the solution to the problem was floating icebergs. He became an enormous nuisance in his attempts to draw attention to his ideas, and eventually died insane.

A controversy erupted between the floating iceberg theorists – who, essentially, were proposing a modification of the old Universal Flood hypothesis – and those few scientists who were attracted to Agassiz's Ice Age glaciers concept. It was settled by the intervention of the British geologist Charles Lyell.

Lyell was one of the most distinguished scientists of his day. His reputation was based on a massive interpretation of geological history entitled *Principles of Geology*, the first volume of which had been published in 1830. In this work, Lyell took issue with virtually every geologist on the planet. Whether by flood, floating ice or divine intervention, there was a clear consensus that what happened to the world had been abrupt, sudden, catastrophic. Lyell maintained it was nothing of the sort.

As Lyell saw it, the causes of geologic change have always been gradual and constant. What is happening today – essentially slow weathering through wind and rain, slow earth movements, slow mountain building – is what has always happened in the past. There might be a few localised aberrations caused by volcanic action, earthquake or flood, but taking things as a whole, there had never been sudden, violent changes.

Although Agassiz himself believed the onset of his Ice Age had been sudden, Lyell did not. In the slow creep of glaciers he saw a reflection of his own uniformitarian ideas. When Lyell threw his massive prestige behind the theory of an Ice Age, Agassiz shut up about catastrophic beginnings. It proved to be a useful trade-off. With Lyell on his side, Agassiz quickly found his ideas were now being treated with profound respect.

Those ideas had become quite spectacular, having progressed far beyond his original observations about Alpine glaciers. He believed that temperatures had plunged repeatedly before the Alpine glaciation and a sea of ice had covered almost all of northern and western Europe, extending down across the western reaches of the Mediterranean into North Africa as far as the Atlas mountains. There were similar immense ice sheets covering north-west Asia and much of North America. Only the topmost peaks of mountain ranges emerged from these vast seas, as solitary islands.

Now he could no longer advocate a catastrophic beginning to his Ice Age, Agassiz made no proposals at all about what had caused the temperatures to plummet in the first place. He simply said the climate changed – which explained nothing.

Once the basic idea started to be taken seriously, scientists began to spot its weaknesses. One of the most glaring was that ice sheets can't move of their own accord. In order to blanket the vast areas of Agassiz's speculations, they had to move down from higher ground.

A new theory arose. This called for the eruption of an extensive range of very high mountains at or near the North Pole. The rise of these mountains pushed accumulated ice downwards and outwards to form the new ice sheets. The Ice Age ended when, for reasons of their own, the Polar mountains disappeared. Agassiz's sea of ice, no longer replenished by fresh supplies from the Arctic, simply melted. Although no one at that time (or since) had discovered the slightest trace of the Polar mountains, their existence was so widely assumed by the scientific community that they came to be taken as an established fact. As was the reality of Agassiz's Ice Age.

The ready acceptance of disappearing mountains was made possible by the fact that Agassiz and others believed their Ice Age to have been a one-off event – something triggered by freak conditions that lasted a limited time, then returned to a warmer normality.

But then a Scots geologist, Andrew Ramsay, announced evidence of not one Ice Age, but two. In Switzerland, botanist Oswald Heer confirmed his findings by discovering deposits which contained the remains of warm-weather plants and animals. He concluded there had to be an 'inter-glacial' period during which they had flourished.

These discoveries proved to be the start of a movement as inexorable as the creep of ice. Successive geologists increased the number of ice ages from Ramsay's two to three or four, then five or six, then seven or more, all with warm inter-glacial periods of greater or lesser duration. Agassiz's relatively moderate proposal had been extended to encompass a 2.5-million-year-long Ice Age punctuated by brief periods of warm or temperate weather.

In the excitement generated by this awesome concept, nobody stopped to wonder why the Polar mountains kept popping up and down like yo-yos.

Although there have been modifications to Agassiz's original vision of vast seas of ice, science today still firmly believes in a Pleistocene Ice Age. Indeed, fresh discoveries have extended the theory beyond anything the Victorian geologists envisaged. 'Ice scour' on Precambrian rock strata has suggested a primeval Ice Age in eastern Asia and the south Pacific. India, Australia, South Africa and South America all seem to have experienced an Ice Age in the Permian. There is localised evidence of glacial spread in the Silurian and Cretaceous. The multiplicity of Ice Ages has made the question of cause all the more urgent, but it is a question that has yet to be answered. There have, of course, been theories.

Astronomers postulate that every 220 to 250 million years the solar system enters one of two space clouds – areas characterised by billions of tiny particles of floating matter. With these particles absorbing solar radiation, it may be that the planet would cool down enough to start an Ice Age.

Another theory holds that a massive increase in sunspots might reduce solar radiation, even if we weren't in a space cloud at the time.

The Yugoslav astronomer, Milutin Milankovich, once took time to compare eccentricities in the Earth's orbit with peculiarities in the inclination of the planetary axis. He found nine points in the last 600,000 years during which he believed the Earth was likely to endure extreme cold. His findings created a stir since they agreed rather well with currently proposed dating of glacier advances during the Pleistocene. The excitement died down when an extension of his calculations failed to show any correlation with earlier Ice Ages.

D. S. Allan and J. B. Delair list eight categories of theory explaining the advent of an Ice Age.[22] These categories are:

1 **Astronomical influence.** Theories in this category vary from meteor bombardment to the solar system's movement into an unusually chill area of space.

2 **Atmospheric change.** Some of the ideas put forward under this heading are of particular relevance to our present age. They include diminished atmospheric carbon dioxide – a sort of reverse greenhouse effect – and/or changes in the ozone layer. Increases in atmospheric dust content (as a result of volcanic activity, for example) would also tend to cut back the amount of heat from the sun reaching our planet.

---

[22] In their comprehensive *When the Earth Nearly Died,* Gateway Books, Bath, 1995.

3 **Axial/Orbital change.** A tilt in the Earth's axis would move certain areas of the planet away from the sun. A lengthening of the orbit would move the whole planet. Both obviously lead to temperature drops.

4 **Geophysical change.** The theory of continental drift, now widely accepted by the scientific community, might just possibly be extended to encompass the idea of land masses drifting into the polar regions, collecting a covering of ice, then drifting out again. Some scientists believe the known movement of the poles – which reflects gradual changes in the Earth's axis of rotation – might in certain circumstances lead to planetary chilling.

5 **Glaciological change.** Here the theorists postulate periodic melting of the underlying layers in the planet's natural ice caps. This would lead to a surge outwards of the upper layers with consequent influence on sea levels.

6 **Land/Water change.** Some theories in this category are variations on the old Polar mountains idea since they suggest the upward movement of massive land areas. Once they breach the snowline, a vast reservoir of ice would naturally form with glaciers sliding down to cover lower-lying districts. Water theories include changes in ocean currents or general circulation or even wholesale relocation of the oceans themselves.

7 **Meteorological change.** Here we are back to Agassiz's bland assertion of a change in climate, without any real attempt to explain why. But in fairness to modern proponents of the theory, a fall in global temperature is now generally thought of as a mechanism for maintaining the ice once it was formed rather than triggering its formation in the first place.

8 **Solar emission change**. This category encompasses the various theories that suggest solar radiation has changed in intensity and/or composition from time to time, thus reducing the amount of heat received by Earth.

It is probably fair to say that while many of the theories show considerable ingenuity, none of them is generally accepted as an adequate explanation of the Ice Age. But their failure is hardly surprising since they are all based on a wrong assumption. This is the assumption that what triggers an Ice Age is cold.

Today, the coldest region on the face of the planet is Siberia. It is colder than Greenland, colder than Antarctica. Yet while Greenland and Antarctica are covered by ice sheets, Siberia is not.

Cold in itself does not lead to glaciation. Once you realise this, it comes as (slightly) less of a surprise to discover that the first prerequisite of an Ice Age is a rise in temperature, not a fall.

For ice to form, you need water. In nature, this water is supplied by rainfall. Rain, in turn, arises out of evaporation from the oceans.

To produce the volume of ice believed to cover the Earth during the Pleistocene Ice Age, ocean levels are calculated to have dropped by as much as 1,000 feet in places. But this drop must have occurred *before* the formation of the ice, not after – something that requires a dramatic rise in world temperature. Although the temperature rise could be gradual, it would have to be followed by a sudden and prolonged period of intense cold to allow the ice sheets to form.

These are bizarre conditions. Ice Age theorists have not the slightest idea how they might have come about.

9

THE ICE AGE MYTH

_____ **FACT** _____

THERE IS NO FORCE ON EARTH THAT WILL CAUSE ICE
TO FLOW UP A MOUNTAIN, OR EVEN A LOW HILL. THE
IDEA IS AS BIZARRE AS AN UPWARD FLOWING STREAM
OF WATER. IN OTHER WORDS, THE MOVEMENT OF ICE
IN THE ICE AGE CONTRADICTS THE LAWS OF PHYSICS.

In 1908, the British lawyer and antiquarian Charles Dawson was fossil hunting in a gravel formation at Barkham Manor, near Lewes, Sussex, when he unearthed the first of a series of finds that included fragments of a skull, jawbone, tooth and other remnants of a prehistoric human. The discoveries were to make him famous.

In 1912, Dawson brought the specimens to Arthur Smith Woodward, keeper of the British Museum's Palaeontology Department. Woodward, in turn, made a formal announcement about them at a meeting of the Geological Society of London on 18 December of that year.

Scientists who examined the relics were delighted. For years, Darwinian evolutionists had struggled with the problem of the 'missing link', the creature assumed to fill the gap between our simian ancestors and modern man. Now it appeared the creature had been found. It was hailed as a breakthrough and named

Eoanthropus dawsoni (Dawson's Dawn Man) in honour of the discoverer.

But in 1926, scientists found the gravels in which *dawsoni* had lain were much more recent than originally supposed. This threw some doubts on the antiquity of the fossil bones themselves – doubts confirmed in 1949 by fluorine dating.

Intensive investigation four to five years later revealed the fossils – today more generally known as Piltdown Man – were not merely misdated, but actually faked. The skull fragment was human, but no more than 50,000 years old. The jawbone belonged to an orang-utan. The tooth had come from a chimpanzee. Chemical tests showed the fragments were deliberately stained. The teeth had been filed to make them look more human.

Although there are other suspects – Woodward, and such celebrities as Sir Arthur Conan Doyle and Teilhard de Chardin have all been considered – Dawson himself is now thought the most likely perpetrator of the fraud. Certainly he had a history of trying to take scientists down a peg or two. Some years before the Piltdown Man announcement, Dawson hauled a sackful of flint into a meeting of his local antiquarian society at Lewes. While his fellow members watched him in amazement, he put it on the floor and began to jump up and down on it. When the flint was well and truly shattered, he opened the sack and shook out the stones. Many of the fragments were absolutely identical to what were then, and still are today, claimed to be ancient hand tools. The scientists of Lewes reacted to this object lesson by snubbing Dawson thereafter.

The idea that scientists can be mistaken does not sit well with the scientific community, however often it is demonstrated.

Every age has its particular paradigm, its way of looking at the world, it consensus opinion of how things are or were. For the whole of the twentieth century, and a sizeable part of the nineteenth, the prevailing paradigm of a Pleistocene Ice Age has been stoutly defended by dismissing, ridiculing, or ignoring evidence to the contrary.

This approach has been so successful it seems almost heresy to suggest the hypothesis of an Ice Age might be just plain wrong. But evidence to the contrary has now mounted to alarming proportions, and field research has shown up enormous cracks in Ice Age theory.

This theory holds that ice sheets and glaciers originated in the frozen north and flowed south. Unfortunately, there are large areas of the frozen north that show no signs of ever having been glaciated.

In the last chapter we noted that Siberia, the coldest region on Earth, has no ice sheet today. There are clear indications that it didn't have an ice sheet in the Ice Age either. Millions of tons of moving ice raze everything in their path. In Siberia, neighbouring Alaska and several Arctic islands even further north, you can find to this day the frozen remains of trees and plants (alongside slim rock pinnacles) that stand in mute testament to the fact that ice sheets never passed their way.

Even where you find signs that ice *did* come, it sometimes didn't come often enough. In southern Scotland, for example, there are indications of glacial action from the very last of the many Pleistocene advances, but nothing from the earlier ones. Even then, the ice that did arrive made almost no difference to the topography of southern Scotland, suggesting that what happened was something substantially less than the millions of tons the theorists suppose.

Oddly enough, south-western Scotland shows less evidence of glacial erosion than surrounding areas. Geologists explain this by the fact that south-west Scotland is generally lower lying than the neighbouring districts. This would explain a lack of glaciation in our present moderate climate. In an Ice Age, the glaciers and ice sheets are supposed to have moved from the high ground to the low ground, leaving the situation in south-west Scotland something of a mystery.

It's not the only Scottish mystery. Aberdeenshire, further north, should, according to theory, have been heavily glaciated. The evidence is that it was never glaciated at all. Worse still, many areas of the North Sea show little or no glacial deposits – an impossibility if we believe an expansion of a Scandinavian ice sheet covered the British Isles.

There's a problem with the erratics as well. Those deposited on the Dogger Bank (a submerged sandbank in the North Sea) were transported from the north-west. If they came with the Scandinavian ice sheet, they would have come from the east. The Outer Hebrides display essentially the same difficulty with their rock striations. These follow the typical pattern in that they run from the north-east to the south-west – hardly what you would expect if they were made by an ice sheet approaching from Scandinavia.

These northern discoveries are only the tip of the proverbial iceberg. Wherever they may have come from, the ice sheets that were supposed to have covered virtually all of the British Isles have left precious few traces. There are large areas of England, Ireland, Scotland and Wales that show no signs of glaciation whatsoever. Even more surprisingly, the Scandinavian ice sheet somehow managed to avoid razing rock spires off the Norwegian coast as it pushed inexorably westward.

The difficulties are compounded when we remember that the mechanics of the Ice Age require the existence of great mountain ranges to act as the ice-making machines that keep things moving. In Europe, the Alpine glaciation that encouraged Agassiz to formulate his Ice Age theory in the first place is now known to have been very limited indeed – and even then almost certainly confined to the last of the proposed glacial advances. Nor is there any longer the possibility that the Alps were a centre for generating appreciable quantities of ice as was formerly supposed. This mountain range reached its present height in relatively recent times – *after* the Ice Age is supposed to have ended. During the Pleistocene itself, the Alps were little more than a chain of low hills. They were too low to generate appreciable quantities of ice.

In fact, it's quite difficult to find any of the mountain ranges that were supposed, in Ice Age theory, to have acted as the focus of glacial expansion. Not only the Alps, but the Rockies and the Himalayas attained their present heights too late to fit the bill.

It gets worse. Examination of glaciated hills and mountains, particularly in North America, typically shows markings only on their northern and north-western slopes. If the mountain in question generated ice on its summit, as high mountains were supposed to do, then the ice would have flowed equally down all slopes, creating glacial scour as it went.

If, on the other hand, the ice sheet approached from the north – which would also fit orthodox theory – then it must gradually have climbed the northern facing slopes. This is fully in accord with the signs. But having reached the top, the ice sheet would then logically slide down the other side, substantially faster because of gravity. This slide would have produced scour on the southern slopes.

The same north–south peculiarity is seen in drift materials. The gravel and erratics carried by the ice sheets typically pile up on the northern sides of mountains. They seem seldom to be deposited on the southern slopes. Ice Age theorists have no explanation for this phenomenon.

Consider the facts:

▲ There are erratics in the Sahara Desert.

▲ There are erratics on the Mongolian Plain.

▲ There are erratics in Uruguay.

▲ There are erratics rammed with great violence into the hill-sides of Labrador, in Canada.

None of these areas – and they are just four examples among many – were ever glaciated. Ice Age theorists have no explain of this either.

The physics of ice is now very well understood. Like any other crystalline solid, it changes shape in response to pressure. This change is elastic. Once you take the pressure off, it returns to its original shape. But that's only the response to short-term pressure. If you apply force to ice for long enough, the change in shape becomes permanent. At this point, ice begins to creep.

Creep involves two processes. One is called *intracrystalline gliding*, in which the layers inside the ice crystals break off parallel to each other but manage not to destroy the continuity of the ice sheet as a whole. The other is known as *recrystallisation*. Here the boundaries of the individual ice crystals change in size or shape without breaking. The nature of this change depends on the way neighbouring crystals are lying and the exact nature of force you are applying. Either way, the ice moves.

The most common force to be applied to large bodies of ice is gravity. You can see this at work in places such as Antarctica and Greenland, where large-scale ice sheets still exist. Generally speaking, the flow of these ice sheets isn't directly out to the sea. What you get is ice moving from high areas (under the influence of gravity) into drainage basins where it concentrates into (relatively) fast-moving streams.

The patterns of these streams obviously differs depending on the actual terrain. East Antarctica, for example, has several high points. Greenland is a ridge with two summits. West Antarctica is a jumble of ridges and troughs so the pattern of its ice streams is chaotic.

Because the surface slope of an ice sheet is extremely small and the ice itself is so cold, flow rates in the interior of an ice sheet are very low – often less than an inch a year. But as the ice moves outward, the rate of flow increases.

Once the flow is channelled into glaciers or ice streams on the outer edges of the sheet, it speeds up dramatically. By the time it hits the ocean, the ice can be travelling at anything up to half a mile a year.

The motive force behind this movement is always gravity. Ice moves forever downhill. But the picture is complicated by heat. Every time you raise the temperature by about 15°C, you increase the rate of creep by a factor of ten. Heat generated by friction – for example the friction generated by the ice moving against bedrock – works the same way.

Obviously there's an upper limit to the supercharging effect of heat. Once the temperature moves above freezing point, ice ceases to be ice and becomes water. At least one Antarctic ice stream moves quite quickly on a layer of water-charged sediment.

The word *glacier* means a river of ice. The fact that glaciers flow at all is a simple consequence of the weight and creep properties of the ice that forms there. As ice builds up in a glacier, a surface slope develops. This slope and the weight of the ice creates internal stresses and creep begins.

Once glaciers reach melting points at their base, they are capable of moving, at least for a limited distance, over flat terrain. Because small bumps and bulges in the bedrock set up stresses in the ice, the glacier will actually move a little faster over rough ground than smooth. Or rather, the *upper layers* of the glacier will move faster. The base layers will not move at all. Furthermore, even the upper layers will not continue to move indefinitely. The pressures that cause ice to move on a flat surface will, at their absolute peak, drive it no more than about 7 miles. Any greater force simply crushes the ice.

There is no force on Earth that will cause ice to flow up a mountain, or even a low hill. The idea is as bizarre as an upward flowing stream of water. In other words, the movement of ice in the Ice Age contradicts the laws of physics.

10
GLOBAL CATACLYSM

——————————— FACT ———————————

WHAT WE ARE EXAMINING HERE IS NOTHING LESS THAN

A MASSIVE CONVULSION OF THE PLANETARY SURFACE –

SO MASSIVE IT ALMOST BEGGARS THE IMAGINATION.

————————————————————————

If it wasn't ice – and clearly it can't have been ice whatever the experts have been telling us – what moved the erratics? This is no trivial question. Stones broken off from the Alps were carried as far as the Jura mountains, on the French-Swiss border. There they lie to this day, their mineral content stark testament to their place of origin. These are not small stones. Many are 1,000 cubic feet or more in size. One is 10,000 cubic feet. Most lie at a height of 2,000 feet or more above Lake Geneva.

Boulders from Scandinavia ended up scattered across Germany, including the higher reaches of the Harz mountains. Huge stones from Finland were swept across Poland and into the Carpathians.

Some erratics are immense. There's one in New Hampshire, USA, weighing 10,000 tons. Another in Ohio covers the better part of an acre and weighs 13,500 tons. But these two put together are pebbles when compared with the monstrous erratics in Britain and Sweden. According to G. F. Wright, a whole village has been built on an erratic that is now bedded down on the east coast of England. Near Malmö, Sweden, a chalk erratic is actually being mined commercially. It is an astonishing 3 miles long.

Although these rocks, and others like them, are known to have travelled hundreds, even thousands, of miles, many of them retain sharp edges. The implication is both unexpected and startling. They had to be transported quickly. A long, slow grind would have worn away the edges.

While something was hurling boulders across the face of the globe, something else was mountain-building.

You very seldom find a solitary mountain. Mostly they come in ranges; and when ranges are linked together, you have what geologists call a mountain belt, such as the Rockies or the Andes.

But it doesn't stop there. All the world's major mountain belts belong to one of two great systems. These are labelled the Circum-Pacific and the Alpine-Himalayan. The grouping is not a category convenience. There seems to be an actual linkage between the mountain belts in these enormous mega-systems.

Mountains are formed in one of four ways. Where magma oozes or erupts upwards from the planet's molten core, the cooling rock forms itself into a cone typical of a volcanic mountain. But most mountains aren't volcanic. The others are formed by folding, faulting, or the warping upwards of the Earth's surface.

Geologists are now fairly certain that the surface of the Earth is made up of enormous plates that float on the molten interior. These plates are in constant motion and while the movement is measured in feet and inches a year, it is still enough to cause stresses that can, in turn, cause quite spectacular geological phenomena. This is especially true where the edges of one gigantic plate meet the edges of another. All of our major mountain systems are believed to have arisen, one way or another, from the interaction of these floating plates.

The process is fairly easy to picture. Imagine two great tectonic plates in collision. It's a long, slow collision, but it's a collision none the less and the sheer size of the massive plates means there's a lot of energy involved. As the plates grind inexorably together, there is greater and greater compression of the rocks at their leading edges. Eventually the inevitable happens. The ground begins to fold upwards and the result is a mountain – or rather, a mountain range.

This is exactly what happened when the plate that holds the Indian subcontinent moved far enough north to make contact with the Eurasian plate. The two pushed, compressed, folded . . . and the result was the Himalayas. Further west, the African plate has been creeping north as well. At some stage in the past, this creep closed off an ancient equatorial ocean (known as the Tethys) leaving only the Mediterranean Sea in its place. It also folded the Alps, the Pyrenees and the Atlas mountains.

The mountains around the Pacific Basin were formed slightly differently. Here, instead of two plates pushing together, one began to slide underneath the other, a process known as subduction. As the leading edge of the Pacific Ocean plates began to undergo this process, some of the rock was carried into the molten core and melted. Pressures then built and the molten rock was thrown up again in the form of lava. This gave rise to a landscape of volcanic cones, like those in the American Cascades or, far more widely, in Japan.

Along other stretches of the Pacific Basin, the crust in the upper of the two plates is too thick to allow much eruption of the molten rock, so mountains form without many, or sometimes any, volcanoes. This is what happened in the Andes of South America.

Secondary factors sometimes come into play. With the Atlas mountains of north-west Africa and the North American Rockies, for example, the collision of the two plates resulted in a shortening of the Earth's crust in one of the plates rather than along the leading edges. The result was much the same, except the mountains arose in a different place.

Mountains usually fall into one of four types: dome, fault-block, fold and volcanic.

Dome mountains arise when the surface of the earth is pushed up without fracturing. This gives a flat surface that gently slopes towards the lowlands. The Black Hills of Dakota, USA, are dome mountains.

Fault-block mountains are what they sound like – mountains made from enormous blocks of the Earth's crust that have been pushed upwards along fracture zones. You can see mountains of this type in America as well – the Sierra Nevadas are excellent examples.

Fold mountains are those we've been talking about and they're exactly what they sound like – mountains literally folded up out of the Earth's crust as a result of the sideways pressure exerted when the tectonic plates collide. The Swiss Juras are fold mountains, as are the Appalachians in North America.

Mountains resulting from volcanic activity are themselves one of two types. One is the ash, cinder and lava cones that arise from active volcanoes. You see examples of these in Japan's Mount Fuji and Hawaii's Mauna Loa. The other is a mountain built from lava solidified in volcanic pipes then eroded to create the final mountain shape. The Cairngorms, in Scotland, are mountains of this type.

What is seldom realised outside geological circles is that the major mountain ranges of our planet are all of recent origin.

The Alps are the great mountain system of south-central Europe, running about 750 miles in an arc from the Gulf of Genoa to

Vienna. They were first formed about 44 million years ago as the result of prolonged tectonic pressures that only really stopped around 9 million years ago. But it would be a mistake to think of them as being formed in anything like the shape, and particularly the height, they are today. According to R. Trümpy's definitive *Geology of Switzerland*[23] the range began as little more than a ridge of low hills in northern Italy, located a considerable distance from where they are today. The shortening of the crust that gave them their present form was, to say the least, extreme. It was no less than 60 miles in length and may even have been as much as 350 miles. Gigantic rock slabs, thousands of feet thick and hundreds of miles long, were pushed up and over the rock strata beneath – a process that continued for a full 100 miles.

Many geological textbooks give the impression (without actually saying so) that this process occurred many millions of years ago and took many more millions of years to complete. This does not seem to be the case.

Today, the two highest Alpine peaks reach a height of more than 15,000 feet. This represents an uplift of the original north Italian hills of somewhere between 12,000 and 13,000 feet. The peaks themselves show little sign of erosion, suggesting that, like the transportation of the erratics, they rose quickly. What we are examining here is nothing less than a massive convulsion of the planetary surface – so massive it almost beggars the imagination.

The convulsion occurred, according to Professor Oswald Heer, 'in the late Pleistocene'.[24] That's around the time something moved the boulders.

---

[23] Basel, 1980.
[24] In *When the Earth Nearly Died*, Gateway Books, Bath, 1995.

The word 'Himalaya' is a combination of two Sanskrit words which mean 'abode of the snows'. It is a perfect description for the Himalaya mountain range which sweeps in a 1,500 mile arc across the northern reaches of the Indian subcontinent and marks the divide between India and Chinese-occupied Tibet. These mountains are the highest in the world. They nowhere drop below 24,000 feet above sea level. The highest mountain of the range (and of the world) is Everest, which towers to a height of more than 29,000 feet.

Apart from their impressive height, the Himalayas are massive. The width of the system varies between 125 and 250 miles. It covers an area of about 229,500 square miles. They are described as 'geologically young'.[25] Just how young can be dated with unusual accuracy since the geological process of their elevation involved a simultaneous rise of some 5,000 to 6,000 feet in the Kashmir Valley. The valley bed contained Pleistocene fossils. Even more directly, the ancient Himalayan rock was folded over Pleistocene gravel beds. The process was not confined to that part of the Himalayas in Kashmir. The Pir Panjal range, which forms part of the western Himalayas at the Punjab, elevated simultaneously. So did the Kailas range, one of the highest and most rugged parts of the Himalayas, located in the south-western part of Tibet. It looks as though the Himalayas rose about the same time as the Alps.

The Alps and Himalayas were not the only mountains to achieve their present elevation at that time.

---

[25] In *Encyclopaedia Britannica*, 1995 edition.

The Hindu Kush is the 500-mile-long mountain system of central Asia that forms a water divide between the Amu Darya and the Indus river valleys. It is neighbour to the Pamir mountains in the east and runs south-west through Pakistan before merging with minor ranges in western Afghanistan. Geological evidence indicates that this range elevated dramatically in the late Pleistocene.

The Altai mountains are a complex system in central Asia extending 1,200 miles from the Gobi Desert to western Siberia. The system has three main branches – the Gobi, Mongolian, and Russian-Kazakh. At its highest point, the system rises to 14,783 feet. Geological evidence indicates this range elevated dramatically in the late Pleistocene.

The Karakorum range runs some 300 miles from Afghanistan into Kashmir and occupies about 80,000 square miles of our planetary surface. It is one of the highest mountain systems in the world, with an average height of about 20,000 feet. Four peaks exceed 26,000 feet in elevation, the highest being K2, the second highest mountain in the world. Geological evidence indicates this range was also elevated dramatically in the late Pleistocene.

The convulsion was not confined to Asia. In North America, the Cascades and Sierra Nevadas rose by more than 6,000 feet. In South America, the Andes elevated as well.

Geologist R. F. Flint sees these various processes as linked. In a definitive survey he suggests a connection between the dramatic elevation of the Alps, the Himalayas, the Cordilleran ranges of North and South America and the Caucausus mountains of Russia.[26]

Interestingly, the formation of the Cordilleran fold seems to be related to the development of submarine trenches along the Pacific reaches of the North American continent. It's as if areas of the seabed were dropping at the same time as mountain ranges

---

[26] *Glacial Geology and the Pleistocene Epoch*, New York, 1947.

were rising. You would almost begin to wonder if Plato could have been right about a sinking continent.

In China, the worldwide mountain-building convulsions of the late Pleistocene were accompanied by a geological event even more spectacular.

The Great Han Hai, as it is known locally, was an inland sea that has long since disappeared. The Han Hai is no myth. Geological investigation has shown the sea occupied what is now the Gobi basin, stretching some 2,000 miles from the Khingan Shan in the east to the Pamirs in the west, with a north-south extent of more than 700 miles. As the 1,500-mile-long Tien Shan range pushed upwards, so did the Han Hai seabed, which raised more than 2,000 feet, draining an almost unimaginable volume of water.

The entire Tibetan plateau rose 9,750 feet to its present height of 14,985 feet. The Yunnan mountain range elevated 6,500 feet. The Bayan Kara Shan range in western China grew by a similar amount. In northern China, massive lava flows erupted in the Great Khingan Shan and Sikhote-Alin ranges. On the country's eastern shoreline, the sea floor collapsed all the way to Japan.

Further afield, near Malaya, the sea level fell by up to 300 feet. There were further mountain elevations in Burma, Thailand, Laos, Vietnam, the Philippines, Indonesia and Australia. In central India, the course of the Narbada River changed.

In Africa, the Earth's crust cracked to form the Great Rift Valley. In New Zealand there was a near unbelievable 58,500 feet uplift on South Island. There was widespread volcanic activity in the islands of the Canaries and the Azores.

There were Old Stone Age fossils in the gravel beds of Kashmir that were underfolded when the mountains rose. There were written records of the Great Han Hai. Humans watched the convulsive elevation of the Himalayas. Humans watched the cataclysmic draining of an ancient sea.

11

QUAKES AND
VOLCANOES

FACT

THERE IS ONLY ONE CONCLUSION POSSIBLE, BUT IT

IS A CONCLUSION ALMOST TOO FANTASTIC TO

CONTEMPLATE. IN VERY, VERY RECENT TIMES INDEED,

THE ATLANTIC SEABED MUST HAVE BEEN ABOVE THE

SURFACE OF THE OCEAN.

Something even more dreadful happened towards the end of the Pleistocene. For reasons not yet clearly understood, whole species disappeared. We lost the mammoth and the mastodon, the sabre-toothed cats and the woolly rhino. Experts have estimated that of all the large-species extinctions in the 2.5 million-year sweep of the Pleistocene, 75 per cent of them occurred during an 800-year period dated around 9000 BC.

We tend to think of species extinctions as gradual affairs, like the long, slow disappearance of the tiger in China, the white rhino in Africa or the wolf in western Europe. But there is evidence that the Pleistocene extinctions were anything but gradual.

To the north of Mount Kinley, Alaska, excavations for gold have unearthed the remains of thousands of animals – mammoth, mastodon, bison and the like – along with vast quantities of uprooted trees. All were frozen in the icy cold. These creatures did not die peacefully. Their bones were twisted, broken and disarticulated. The trees were splintered. They must have been intermingled by some violent prehistoric catastrophe of almost unimaginable magnitude.

It was not a local catastrophe. The remains were discovered in a layer of frozen silt. Similar silts with a burden of animal remains have been found in the Yukon, on the Koyukuk river to the north, and on the Kuskokwim river that feeds into the Bering Sea. More still have been unearthed at several sites along the Arctic coast.

The animals buried in these silts did not die alone. Yuma points – worked flints used as arrowheads and spears – were found at various levels 100 or more feet below the surface. Human hunters perished with their prey.

The explorers who landed on the New Siberian Islands in 1805 found their soil 'packed full' of the bones of elephants and rhinoceroses in 'astonishing numbers'. The hunter Liakhov, who gave his name to the island he explored north of Siberia (and some 600 miles inside the Arctic Circle) discovered so many mammoth remains that he began to wonder if the island might not actually be composed of them, cemented together by icy sand.

A similar picture emerges in far warmer climes. During the first six months of archaeological excavation, 20 tons of hippo bones were excavated from the San Ciro cave near Palermo, Sicily. These were not ancient fossils millions of years old. The bones were so recent they were sent to Marseilles to provide charcoal for the sugar factories there.

There is an archaeological pattern on Sicily of hippopotamus bones packed in their thousands into caves and rock fissures, despite the fact that hippos never live in this type of habitat. Often their bones are mingled with those of lion, hyena, bear and elephant, as if all these animals had been somehow thrown together in the caves to die.

Several of the Sicilian sites contain puzzles in the form of two species, *Hippopotamus pentlandi* and *Palaeoloxodon mnaidriensis*, which were not thought to have been native to the island. But if not native, then these creatures would have had to be transported from Malta, Crete, Cyprus, Greece or northern Italy in order to deposit their bones where they were found. On Malta itself, one site excavated in the nineteenth century produced the bones of elephants, lizards, giant birds, turtles and a species of enormous dormouse, all now extinct. These skeletons were intermingled with huge stone blocks and boulders. The smashed and shattered bones clearly indicated they had died violently. The remains of the turtles, trapped between the rocks or jammed into fissures, were another puzzle. As water creatures, they had to be transported from some other as yet unidentified locality. Another Maltese site produced a fissure packed with the remains of elephants, birds and, astoundingly, sharks.

Limestone caves on Crete are also packed with the jumbled bones of Pleistocene animals ranging from elephants through deer to pygmy hippopotami and rodents. Essentially the same situation has arisen with the archaeological exploration of Corsica, Sardinia and the Balearics.

On the Arctic island of Cérigo, residents refer to a 'mountain of bones' in describing a truncated mound located near Cérigo village which has its surface and many cracks and fissures literally bristling with the remains of Pleistocene fauna.

On the Rock of Gibraltar, fissures are packed with the smashed and splintered bones of hyena, lynx, various birds, rhino, wolf, boar, deer, ibex, ox, panther, hare and rabbit. Although predator and prey species are jumbled together there is no indication of specific kills. These animals died together – and died suddenly. Their remains have been excavated by the ton.

A single cave in Yorkshire, England, yielded the remains of

elephants, rhinos, horses, hippos, bears, wolves, hyenas, hares, tigers, ravens, pigeons, snipe, ducks and larks. Three caves at Oreston, near Plymouth, excavated in the early 1800s, were packed with similar remains. Kent's Cavern, near Torquay, provided particularly vivid evidence that Pleistocene animals and birds had been forced into the caves with extreme violence, but there were clear signs of violence in virtually all other sites as well.

There are bone caves of this type in Germany, France, Italy, Austria, Croatia, Poland and the former Czechoslovakia. More have been discovered in the Lebanon, in Syria and other sites in the Middle East. There are more still in Russia and continental Asia.

In a cavern near the Chinese village of Choukoutien (a short distance from Beijing) the animal bones were mingled with the remains of seven humans representing three diverse racial types – European, Melanesian and Eskimo. Even more bewildering, Vallonet cave, between Monaco and the Italian border, yielded the remains of whales among the bones of lions, rhinos, monkeys, elephants and hyenas.

Australia has its caverns packed with Pleistocene remains. You will find them near Wellington, on the Macleay River, near the head of the Colo River, at Yesseba and several other sites. As elsewhere in the world, the animals were obviously subjected to great violence, with their bones fractured and splintered.

The picture is repeated in South America with packed caves and fissures discovered across Brazil. In North America, there are bone caves in New Mexico, Pennsylvania, and Nevada. Bishop's Cap cave in the Oregon mountains produced a chaos of human bones mingled with those of wolf, horse, bison, coyote, camel, antelope and ground-sloth.

A hugely disturbing picture is emerging from this evidence. It is a picture of an extraordinarily violent planet-wide event that caused widespread geological upheavals, raised mountains, drained at least one sea and slaughtered animals in their millions.

Is it possible that such an event might have been of sufficient violence to submerge a continent?

Plato described the end of Atlantis in the following terms:

> At a later time there were earthquakes and floods of extraordinary violence, and in a single dreadful day and night, all your [Athenian] fighting men were swallowed up by the earth and the island of Atlantis was similarly swallowed up by the sea and vanished; this is why the sea in that area is to this day impassable to navigation, which is hindered by mud just below the surface, the remains of the sunken island.[27]

The reference to the destruction of the Athenian armies suggests this was no local disaster. Coincident with Atlantis disappearing, there were earthquakes on the Greek mainland sufficiently violent to disrupt the very fabric of Athenian society – perhaps even destroy it altogether. Since historical records insist the foundation of the Greek city-state was many thousands of years *after* the date assigned by Plato, the suspicion arises that the Athens we know about was not the original Athens, but a much later revival of a city buried in prehistoric times.

Traditionally, this has been a difficult suspicion to support. Although the earthquakes are described as 'extraordinary', they would actually have to be unprecedented to wipe away all traces of an entire civilisation. For not only did Atlantis disappear, but the prehistoric Greek states, and the Egyptian kingdom supposed to have been in place at that time, all went with it.

---

[27] Plato's *Timaeus*, Desmond Lee translation, Penguin Classics, London, 1971.

The orthodox theory of prehistory, with its insistence on an Ice Age, has no room at all for the picture Plato paints. All modern experts are convinced it is impossible for an entire continent to sink. But the gathering evidence of widespread geological disturbance at the end of the Pleistocene suggests Plato may just possibly have been as accurate in this aspect of his story as he was in so many others. The time may have come to take a second look at the impossible.

The seabed around the Azores is covered in lava of a type technically known as tachylite. It is a substance that weathers quickly. Under water (and indeed in the air) the original black, glassy material turns into something called palagonite, a red, brown, or yellow crystalline material. The change makes a useful, if limited, clock. The tachylite around the Azores is still black. This means the lava erupted no more than 13,000 years ago and may have been substantially more recent.

The Azores lie on the eastern slopes of the Mid-Atlantic Ridge, an immensely long submarine mountain chain that runs for about 10,000 miles in a curving path from the Arctic Ocean close to the southern tip of Africa. It is surrounded by flat seabed plains that run all the way to the continental coasts.

The mountains that make up the ridge are extremely broad as well as long. In places they are 1,000 miles wide and sometimes reach heights that bring them above sea level, forming islands such as the Azores, Ascension, St Helena and Tristan da Cunha.

The geological processes that formed the ridge are ongoing. Along its crest is a long valley varying in width from 50 to 75 miles. On the floor of the valley, molten magma from beneath the Earth's crust continuously wells up to cool then gets pushed away by pressure of the continuing eruptions. This too suggests changes in relatively recent times.

In 1949, the *National Geographic* magazine reported on a marine expedition that made echo-soundings in the area. These showed thousands of feet of sediment deposited on the foothills of the ridge. But when the ship moved away from the ridge and began to take soundings of the ocean basins on either side, an astonishing development occurred.

The scientists began their work quite confident that the sedimentary layers would be even thicker since the Atlantic seabed had lain undisturbed for aeons. But the sediments weren't thicker than those deposited on the relatively recent Mid-Atlantic Ridge. Nowhere did the basin sediments reach a depth of more than 100 feet. In some areas there were no sediments at all.

There is only one conclusion possible, but it is a conclusion almost too fantastic to contemplate. In very, very recent times indeed, the Atlantic seabed must have been above the surface of the ocean.

How did it happen? The answer is far from clear. About 50,000 noticeable earthquakes rumble across the world each year.[28] An astonishing 49,900 of them are too small to be of any real trouble. The remaining 100 are big enough to cause substantial damage, but only if they happen near population centres. Really major earthquakes occur at the rate of about one a year. They hit the headlines when they destroy people or property, but otherwise warrant only an inside paragraph.

There have been several historical occasions when the centre

---

[28] There are actually more. The figure quoted does not include those that can only be detected by instruments.

of a major earthquake lay at, or near, a centre of human population. On 1 November 1755, the Portuguese capital Lisbon was struck by an enormous quake centred some distance off the coast. The quake was so violent that damage was reported in Algiers, more than 600 miles away. It generated tidal waves that pounded Martinique 3,700 miles away. Those waves towered to a height of 20 feet at Lisbon and 65 feet at Cádiz, Spain.

The resultant damage was spectacular. Twelve thousand of Lisbon's houses were destroyed as were most of its large public buildings and churches. Sixty thousand people perished, a figure that includes those who drowned in the tidal waves or burned in the fire that raged for six days after the event.

New Madrid in southern Missouri was hit by three huge earthquakes back-to-back on 16 December 1811, 23 January 1812, and 7 February of the same year. The largest demolished chimneys in Cincinnati, 370 miles away. And then came the aftershocks: 1,874 were felt in Louisville, Kentucky, 180 miles distant. The ground trembled in Canada.

Some 38,600 square miles of ground were shaken violently. In one region, 150 miles long by 37 miles wide, the ground sank to a depth of 10 feet, then was flooded by a local river. Whole forests fell.

Perhaps the most famous earthquake of the twentieth century occurred on 18 April 1906, when, just after five o'clock in the morning, the San Andreas Fault slipped. The resultant quake was felt from California to Oregon. Despite the spread of damage – San Jose, Salinas and Santa Rosa were all hit – the disaster became known as the San Francisco earthquake. Some 700 people were killed in that city, and a fire started which gutted the business district.

Japan is earthquake territory – so much so that traditional housing is wood frame and paper so that collapse does the minimum of damage to occupants. In modern times, however, brick or reinforced concrete has become the material of choice, particularly in urban areas. When, on 1 September 1923, a massive earthquake struck the Tokyo-Yokohama metropolitan area, 54 per cent of brick buildings and 10 per cent of reinforced concrete – amounting to hundreds of thousands of structures – promptly collapsed. The death toll was estimated at more than 140,000. The shock started a tsunami (tidal wave) that reached a height of 40 feet and killed more than 60 people.

On 27 March 1964, a quake that released twice the energy of the San Francisco earthquake occurred in south-central Alaska. This one was felt across an area of 500,000 square miles. Although the death toll was relatively small (131 people perished) the destruction caused was remarkable. A land area of at least 46,000 square miles was actually tilted. Hills were thrust up as high as 80 feet while in other areas land sank as much as 8 feet. There were underwater landslides and tidal waves that caused damage as far away as California. Aftershocks were numbered in tens of thousands.

China almost lost an entire city in 1976 when, on 28 July, a massive quake struck T'ang-shan, about 60 miles east of Peking. The death toll exceeded 240,000.

Disasters though they were, it is quite evident that none of these massive earthquakes came anywhere near destroying whole cultures or sinking whole continents. The huge loss of life and property at T'ang-shan arose because the majority of its buildings were not sufficiently well reinforced to withstand quake damage. Even so, T'ang-shan city still exists today. It was only *nearly* destroyed and has now been rebuilt.

Perhaps the closest quake to Plato's description was the Alaskan in 1964. Here land sank and land was thrust up. Huge tidal waves were formed. Yet even this apocalyptic picture is a pale shadow of the cataclysm Plato described. Historical experience shows us a huge weakness in Plato's story. Earthquakes can't change the world or wipe out whole cultures. They simply don't get big enough to sink Atlantis.

But what about volcanic action? The ground shakes when volcanoes erupt. Perhaps this is what Plato really meant by earthquakes.
Since the late 1700s volcanoes have caused about 250,000 deaths,
70 per cent of them in only four eruptions.

On 8 May 1902, Mont Pelée blew. It was not a particularly
spectacular eruption. Less than a cubic mile of magma poured
from this volcano on the Caribbean island of Martinique. But
much of it formed a high-velocity avalanche that roared down a
steep valley to the port of St Pierre There was no time to evacu-
ate, almost no warning at all in fact. In a matter of minutes, the
entire town was engulfed. A total of 29,000 people died. Pelée
was the worst volcanic disaster of the twentieth century in
terms of lives lost. The second worst occurred on 13 November
1985.

Nevado del Ruiz is a 17,700-foot-high ice-capped volcano in
Colombia. A brief eruption dumped several million cubic yards
of hot lava on the ice around the summit. This had the result of
sending a sudden surge of meltwater down the mountain. The
meltwater in turn created massive mud flows. Much of the town
of Armero, 30 miles east of the mountain, was buried. The death
toll was enormous: 22,000 inhabitants lost their lives.

Perhaps the most famous eruption of all time was that of
Krakatoa on a small, uninhabited Indonesian island between
Sumatra and Java. It occurred on 26–27 August 1883, and produced some spectacular results. When the explosive eruption was
over, Krakatoa collapsed in on itself forming a crater that was
partially below sea level. Almost 10 square miles of the island disappeared altogether, and where a 1,500-foot-high mountain once
stood there was water to a depth of 900 feet. The sound of the
eruption was heard in Australia, 3,000 miles away. A 100-foot-
high tidal wave killed 36,000 people living on the coastlines of

Java and Sumatra. A 50-mile-high ash cloud caused spectacular sunsets worldwide for several years.

Krakatoa is often described as the most violent volcanic explosion in recorded history, but this is in error. The largest eruption of modern times occurred at Tambora volcano on Sumbawa Island, Indonesia, on 10–11 April 1815.

Thirty cubic miles of magma were expelled in a series of massive explosions. More than an inch of ash fell across much of Indonesia and the Java Sea. Before the eruption, Tambora was 14,000 feet high. Afterwards, 4,500 feet of the summit were missing. In their place was a collapsed caldera 3.7 by 4.3 miles wide, and half a mile deep. There were about 10,000 direct deaths from the eruption and subsequent tidal waves, but the thick ash deposits caused widespread crop failure resulting in an additional 82,000 deaths from famine.

On average, volcanoes are responsible for about $100 million worth of property damage a year, but this can vary dramatically on a case-by-case basis. When America's Mount St Helens blew in 1980, for example, the resultant property damage was estimated at $1 billion, although the eruption itself was classified as moderate.

Very often volcanoes can produce more fireworks than damage. Mauna Loa in Hawaii – a densely populated island chain – is the largest volcano in the world. On 25 March 1984, after a year of grumbling, it finally erupted. A fissure split the 3-mile axis of the summit caldera and lava fountains formed a curtain of fire. Observation flights were immediately ordered by the authorities and initial reports showed much of the caldera floor was covered by a lake of molten rock. A black crust quickly formed, riddled by a glowing web of cracks that showed the red-orange incandescent material bubbling below.

The first eruption took place just after one in the morning. By dawn the summit fissure started to enlarge itself down the north-east side of the mountain. A new lava flow began. Two hours later the fracture broke through another 4 miles lower down. Another curtain of fire arose, more than 1 mile long. The vents formed by these gigantic cracks continued to erupt throughout the early afternoon, sending lava down the high south-east flank of the mountain. Around four in the afternoon, a series of earthquakes signalled the opening of new vents further down.

The lava flow from the lower cracks was dramatic. It fountained 60 feet high at a rate of 17.6 million cubic feet an hour. In one day, the flow had travelled 7 miles, moving steadily towards the city of Hilo. The eruption continued with the same ferocity for the next ten days, but the advance of the lava flow slowed down. The second day saw it halved from 7 miles to 4, and halved again on the fourth day. By the time the eruption finished on 15 April, the longest lava flows had travelled 17 miles, just 6 miles from the outskirts of Hilo. Some 7.7 billion cubic feet had spewed from the volcano to cover a total area of 18 square miles. But for all the sound and fury, no one was hurt, and the only significant damage was the cutting of power lines.

There are many hazards associated with volcanic eruption, ranging from the obvious lava flows to the production of toxic clouds. Massive explosions occur in which large blocks can be hurled as far as 12 miles. Gas clouds can suffocate people and scorch vegetation at even greater distances. Ash falls can ruin crops and even collapse roofs. Volcanic eruption can trigger avalanches and mud slides, generate tidal waves and earthquakes. Lava flows bury everything they reach.

Although Tambora was the most explosive volcano in historical times, there is no doubt that eruptions can get larger. Geological investigation suggests that 2 million years ago a volcano at Yellowstone, USA, erupted with such ferocity that it produced sixty times more magma than that coughed up by Tambora.

Experts still insist the greatest hazard is human complacency.

Far too many people living near volcanoes are lulled into a sense of false security between eruptions and often fail to read the all too obvious signs when another one is due.

Scientists have long assured us that while volcanic action is capable of destroying (or indeed creating) a small island, there is no known geological mechanism that will sink a large one. Whatever may have finished Atlantis, destroyed a worldwide culture and changed the face of our planet, you can be quite sure it wasn't volcanic action. But if it wasn't earthquakes and it wasn't volcanoes, what was it?

12

CHANGING CLIMATE

_____ F A C T _____

THERE IS A BODY OF EVIDENCE TO SUGGEST THE

WORLD *WAS* ONCE MORE UPRIGHT AND A CHANGE OF

AXIAL TILT *DID* ACTUALLY OCCUR.

The Earth's orbit is not a circle, but an ellipse. At certain times of the year it approaches closer to the sun, at others it moves further away. Many people imagine it is the form of the orbit that determines the season – winter arrives when the Earth is further from the sun – but this is not the case.

As well as orbiting the sun, the Earth spins on its own axis. But this axis is not at right angles to the plane of the orbit. It actually tilts at an angle of 23.5°. It is this tilt that produces the seasons since it governs the angle at which sunlight strikes our planet and also the comparative lengths of day and night. There is evidence the angle of tilt was not always as it is today.

The zodiac is an imaginary belt in the sky, extending about 8° on either side of the apparent path of the sun among the stars. Its width seems originally to have been fixed in order to include the orbits of the sun and moon plus Mercury, Venus, Mars, Jupiter and Saturn – the five planets visible to the naked eye.

The zodiac is divided into twelve 30° sections called signs, each named for the actual constellation you could see in it if you happened to be watching the sky around 200 BC. Today, although the names of the signs – Aries through to Pisces – are familiar from every newspaper horoscope, the constellations themselves are in different places. This is because the stars appear to move in a 26,000-year cycle which has now brought the constellation Pisces into the sign of Aries, with similar displacements elsewhere. Wait about 24,000 years and the signs will once again agree with the actual constellations.

The origins of the zodiac are very old. It is known to have been used in ancient Babylon, in about 2000 BC, but may well have been developed more than 3,000 years earlier. It proved such a useful convention that it was adopted by the Egyptians and Greeks, and was even developed, apparently independently, by the Aztecs.

Early astronomy (the study of the stars) was not separate from astrology (the prediction of events from planetary positions) as it is today, so the original zodiac would have involved accurate stellar observation.

In the nineteenth century, the astronomer Richard Proctor made an analysis of the ancient zodiacal 'water' constellations – Cancer, Scorpio and Pisces – and concluded that at the time they were devised, the axis of celestial rotation must have differed from what it is today. In 1975, a more expansive astronomical study, published in *Nature* by M. Noel and D. H. Tarling, showed that in 10,178 BC, the celestial pole was inclined at a 30° angle from its present position. Astronomical observations are always relative, so that noted change in the celestial pole might be just as easily – and rather more logically – seen as a 30° shift in our own planetary axis.

The reason for this is curious, but seldom discussed in the texts on astrophysics. Early philosophers assumed the planetary orbits around the sun must be circular, and the axis of rotation must be perpendicular to the orbital plane. When direct astronomical observation showed that this was not the case, the findings were dismissed as blasphemous since they suggested God had been less than perfect in His creation of the solar system.

The real issue, however, has never been God, but the laws of Newtonian physics. The planets orbit the sun because they are tethered to it, so to speak, by gravity. Their motion is governed by exactly the same mechanics as swinging a tethered ball around your head. But if you *have* ever swung a tethered ball around your head, you'll notice it describes a circle – it can't do anything else. Furthermore, the forces which spin the planets around the sun would, in a purely mechanical universe, tend to produce a perpendicular axis of rotation. Thus the idea of a more 'upright' Earth is far from unreasonable.

But if the Earth really was more upright once, it's difficult to see why its axis of tilt would suddenly change. So difficult, in fact, that any suggestions that it did have been largely ignored by the scientific community, which prefers to assume the planet was always much as it is today. This is a pity, since there is a body of evidence to suggest the world *was* once more upright and a change of axial tilt *did* actually occur. But to understand it, you need to know what the world would have been like with a different axis of rotation.

If the recently discovered shift in the celestial pole does reflect a recent change in the angle of the Earth's axis, then the world in which Plato located his lost Atlantis would have been very different to the world we know today.

First of all, the climate would have been far more genial. There would not have been the extremes of summer and winter experienced today. Year round – and worldwide – the climate would have been more temperate. Such a climate produces abundant plant growth, so that the idea of two harvests in a single year no longer seems outlandish. Luxuriant vegetation supports more wildlife, particularly large browsers like the elephant herds Plato claimed roamed the broad plains of Atlantis.

As a consequence of the temperate climate, the polar ice caps would have been far smaller than they are today – and might not have formed at all. It is likely that the chill and barren lands of the Arctic and Antarctic would have been temperate at worst, and may even have been warm. Given decent soil, they could also have been extremely fertile.

With smaller (possibly even non-existent) ice caps at the Poles, sea levels would have been higher in many parts of the globe. The seas themselves would certainly have been calmer, since the engine that drives our planetary weather would have been in an entirely different gear. This would lead to far less frequent storms. In fact, there would have been less rain altogether.

But this is not to envisage drought. An intensely vigorous biosphere is self-sustaining. It produces higher carbon dioxide and oxygen contents in the atmosphere. Humidity would almost certainly have been extremely high – so much so that desert areas were probably quite rare. A typical day would have been one of warmth and sunshine and abundance. Such conditions have cultural implications. The development of a prehistoric civilisation might, in some ways, have been easier than it was in our own era. Wherever it arose, almost anywhere on Earth, there would have been sounder economic underpinnings. And the civilisation itself may have been gentler, more philosophical. It is always easier to think profound thoughts on a full stomach.

One can also envisage a time of peace. Where food, both plant and animal, is plentiful and warmth a worldwide phenomenon, there is little reason for territorial competition. War would have been unusual, for extensive periods probably non-existent.

Then this is the type of world we might expect if the planetary axis was more upright in the Pleistocene era than it is today. In many ways it resembles the idyllic Gold Age described in humanity's diverse mythologies.

Hebrew mythology, adopted by Christianity, describes our first ancestors as living an idyllic existence before disobedience to God caused them to be driven from Eden. The biblical account of this earthly paradise contains a few interesting coincidences when compared with our logical reconstruction of life prior to 10,000 BC.

According to Genesis, 'And out of the ground made the Lord God to grow every tree that is pleasant to the sight, and good for food.'[29] The same source speaks of an Earth that 'brought forth grass, and herb yielding seed after his kind, and the tree yielding fruit'[30] – all suggestive of a time when plant growth was profuse and varied.

Interestingly, the changed climatic pattern is recorded. There is mention of the reduced precipitation – 'the Lord God had not caused it to rain upon the Earth'[31] – and the high humidity – 'there went up a mist from the Earth, and watered the whole face of the ground'.[32] When humanity appears, the world is so benign it is like a garden.

In the West, this is our most familiar allusion to a prehistoric Golden Age but the legend itself is universal. In 700 BC, the

---

[29] Gen. 2:9.
[30] Gen. 1:12.
[31] Gen. 2:5.
[32] Gen. 2:6.

Greek poet Hesiod wrote of a time when people lived without working.[33] They were fed by an Earth so bountiful that agriculture was unnecessary. Long before the Greeks, the Sumerians had described Dilmun, as a land of good water where crops were plentiful. It was in many ways similar to the Egyptian Aalu, another mythological paradise.

The first of four prehistoric kingdoms of Iran was established at a time of peace and plenty. The first age of Hindu mythology, the Krita Yuga, was a prehistoric era noted for its benevolence. Virgil, who believed the Golden Age would return as part of a natural cycle, also envisaged a world in which crops would grow without anybody having to look after them.

Curiously enough, when one remembers Plato, the prehistoric paradise was often located in the Atlantic. Ireland's St Brendan the Navigator was supposed to have found it in the western reaches of that ocean during his seven-year voyage of exploration in the sixth century. St Brendan's Isle, otherwise known as the Island of Blest, and sometimes associated with the equally mysterious Hi Brasil, was described as a land of apples and blossom.

In Greek mythology, the Islands of the Blessed – a concept accepted by many other ancient peoples – were said to be located 'in the west where the sun sets', another expression denoting the Atlantic. An earlier associated Greek concept – that of the Elysian Fields – also located the earthly paradise far to the west. Homer's description is particularly interesting in that he insists it was a land without snow, cold or rain and peopled by humans rather than the spirits of the dead.

You would not be the first person faced with these myths to wonder whether they represented something other than poetic fictions. Could they be distorted memories of the world as it once was, before a shift in the terrestrial axis – and in some cases actual memories of Atlantis itself? But however suggestive myths

---

[33] Hesiod *Works and Days.*

may be, they are not hard evidence. For that we have to turn elsewhere.

The Spitsbergen archipelago is a chain of Norwegian islands in the Arctic Ocean. Its location at 78° 56' north latitude leaves it 1,000 miles within the Arctic Circle. Its summers are cold, with temperatures barely crawling above freezing. Its winters are brutal. Temperatures of minus 40°C are not uncommon. Apart altogether from the winter deep freeze, such an enormous seasonal variation plays havoc with plant life. The range of vegetation that can survive on Spitsbergen is limited – but there are coral reefs in the icy waters off its coast.

Coral is the skeletal remains of tiny sea creatures that survive only in tropical waters. Even sweltering climates, like those of Egypt or Morocco, do not quite raise the temperature high enough to produce it.

In his *Flora Artica Fossilis*, the Dutch botanist O. Heer identified no fewer than 136 species of fossil plants on Spitsbergen, including pines, firs, cypresses, elms, hazels, spruces and even delicate water lilies and tropical palms. At the northernmost tip of the archipelago is a seam of coal that varies from 25 to 30 feet thick, covered in a layer of shale and sandstone that is studded with plant fossils.

Coal is formed when a primeval forest dies and geological pressures cause the ancient wood to change. This is the only way that coal is formed. Its presence on Spitsbergen proves absolutely that there was a time when lush woodland grew within 18° 15' of the North Pole.

Spitsbergen is not unique. There is ancient coral in Alaska, Canada and Greenland. Antarctica, now buried beneath a vast ice sheet, also has coal deposits and fossil wood, indicating a time when it too was forested. As long ago as the 1860s, fossil remains of magnolia and fig were discovered in the north of Greenland.

On Disko Island off the Greenland coast, there is evidence of pine cones, acorns and other varieties of temperate plants. Throughout vast stretches of the Arctic come discoveries of walnut, beech, lime, poplar, oak, magnolia, cypress, holly, dogwood, hawthorn, breadfruit and even tropical ferns.

Iceland has clays containing the remains of sequoia, spruce, oak and maple trees normally associated with sunny California. Banks Island in the Canadian Arctic has yielded finds of acorns, despite the fact that the nearest oak trees are (now) hundred of miles away. It also has frozen wood and fossil trees in great number.

Writing about the discovery of the North West Passage, Robert McClure reports frozen, unfossilised trees on Prince Patrick Island, located at 76° 12' north latitude. There are enormous accumulations of unfossilised and carbonised wood along the Arctic shores of Siberia and along the coastlines of the Bering Strait – so much so we seem to be looking at the remains of entire forests of sequoia, poplar, alder and sycamore . . . all trees that today will only grow far further south.

The implication of these various discoveries is obvious. There was a time when our northlands – not to mention the vast southern reaches of icy Antarctica – must have been warmer, perhaps even a great deal warmer, than they are today. The question is, at what time?

The usual answer is the Miocene, a geological era that began 25 million years ago and ended 5 million years ago. But there's a problem with this attribution. The problem relates to the evolution of plants. If you examine an area in which the climate has changed from, say, temperate to Arctic, over a period of several million years, the fossil record of vegetable life reflects the gradual transition as plants adapt to the new conditions.

There is no such pattern in the fossil record of our northlands. In study after study, fossils attributed to the Miocene have proven virtually indistinguishable from modern species. Millions of years of temperature change apparently produced no changes in the plant life whatsoever.

Mammoths are one of the extinct class of elephants that roamed every continent, except Australia and South America, until about 10,000 years ago. The northern mammoth is the best known of the species, largely because finds of perfectly preserved carcasses in the natural deep-freeze of Siberia have provided a great deal of information about the creature and how it lived. There must have been a great many mammoths in Siberia. In medieval times, the export of their ivory to China and Europe was a major industry.

Many mammoths had a woolly, inch-thick, yellowish brown undercoat beneath a coarser outer covering of dark brown hair that grew up to 20 inches long. For the better part of a century, this shaggy coat was looked on as an adaptation to the biting cold. Today, some scientists aren't quite so sure. They speculate that the woolly coat no more points to cold-weather adaptation than the fur of the tiger in sub-tropical India.

Mammoths, like their kissing cousins the elephants, were vegetarians; and heavy-duty vegetarians at that. Their huge bulk required massive quantities of fodder — fodder that could only have come from an abundance of plant life. Mammoth remains have been found throughout our northlands and throughout the countries that were supposed to have been gripped by the massive glaciation of the Ice Age.

One wonders what they lived on. The plant cover needed to feed the mammoths — and the many other game species that shared their habitat — would only grow in temperate climes.

The evidence of ancient plant life in the Arctic has generated another puzzle. Temperate plants need more than heat to grow. They survive by the process of photosynthesis, and that needs sunlight. Warm-weather plants, such as magnolia and fig, require a lot of sunlight. The remains of lime trees found in Arctic America still had actual limes attached. The fruiting process needs a lot of sunlight too.

Arctic winters are six months long. There simply isn't enough sunlight available to generate the sort of plant growth the fossil record shows. This means that even if you somehow warmed up the polar regions, it would not lead to the plant growth that took place.

Only a shift in the planetary axis solves all the mysteries of our northlands. If Earth rotated in a more upright position, you would no longer have the six-month-long Arctic winter. Consequently, there would be more sunlight available for plant growth. Even quite close to the Poles (both North and South) there would have been a temperate climate.

13

THE OUTER SPACE CONNECTION

_____ FACT _____

THE PICTURE THAT HAS BEEN EMERGING IS CLEAR. IT IS

A PICTURE IN WHICH SUDDENLY, CATASTROPHICALLY,

LAND AND SEA CHANGE PLACES. IT IS A PICTURE OF A

GIGANTIC, UNIVERSAL FLOOD.
_____

The astronomical findings that point to a shift in the Earth's axis suggest it happened recently, sometime around the end of the Pleistocene era. But if it happened recently, it also happened violently. There simply has not been time for a gentle geological tilting. There is no sign of such a gradual process today, no record of it in astronomical observations dating back more than 6,000 years. When the Earth moved, it moved suddenly. And that means it moved catastrophically.

With the key of an axis shift, various pieces of a complex jig-saw begin to come together. There is evidence of a dramatic change in the temperature of the polar regions. This change was not gradual. Mammoths preserved in the Siberian permafrost had fresh grass in their stomachs. They died before they had the opportunity to digest their final meal. These creatures were flash-frozen where they stood.

There is evidence of planetary-wide tectonic disturbance. Every major mountain chain we know today reached its present elevation at the end of the Pleistocene. This represents an upsurge of geological forces that is literally unprecedented. Only something as radical as a planetary cause is sufficient to explain it.

There is evidence of sudden mass extinctions. Species after species perished, not gradually but in an evolutionary eye-blink. They were not confined to a single geological location. Something managed to kill animals by their millions right across the globe. Something so brutal, so violent that it often carried them far from their native habitat and smashed their shattered bodies into caverns and rock fissures.

The same force, we must presume, moved the erratics. It had sufficient energy to lift and transport stone slabs miles long and hundreds of thousands of tons in weight. And these stones, it is now quite clear, were not carried at the slow creep of ancient ice, but hurled across the landscape with the speed of an express train.

If a shift in axis triggered this catastrophe, the time has come to face up squarely to the immediate agent of destruction.

It is known that an ocean once covered what is now northern Germany, central Europe and vast tracts of Russia and China. Geologists have named it the Miocene Ocean, but while it certainly existed in that distant era, analysis of marine fossils and other fauna has led some scientists to believe it disappeared in the relatively recent Pleistocene, which ended only 10,000 years ago. We have already seen that China's inland sea, the Great Han Hai, drained at much the same time.

Analysis of the distribution of flora has led to the presumption that a Pacific continent existed at some stage in deep prehistory. Given names like Gondwanaland, Oceana and Pacifica, it is generally supposed to have disappeared many millions of years ago. But here again the evidence suggests differently.

Botanist Joseph Hooker, who concluded that most of the islands in the Indian Ocean represented the peaks of a lost continent, saw in the distribution of certain conifers a clear indication that Fiji, New Zealand, Tasmania and Australia were once part of the same landmass. His conclusions are supported by the remains of extensive forestation found on the seabed between Panama and the Galapagos Islands, as well as Fiji itself. These forest trees are not ancient species. The land that bore them seems only to have disappeared in late Pleistocene times.

A similar analysis based on the geographical area of the Atlantic shows almost 500 plant species in the Azores are identical, or closely related, to plant species in Europe, Madeira and the Canaries. There is a further connection between plants in Madeira and those found in the West Indies and tropical South America. To explain these connections, several scientists have suggested the existence, again in relatively recent times, of an island chain stretching across the ocean like Plato's Atlantis island empire.

All these landmasses are now gone, drowned by an encroaching sea. The picture that has been emerging is clear. It is a picture in which suddenly, catastrophically, land and sea change places. It is a picture of a gigantic, universal flood.

Every Jewish and Christian child is brought up learning about a prehistoric flood. It came about when God noticed how corrupt humanity had become and decided to destroy the species. But he made an exception of one righteous man, Noah, who built a huge wooden ship to save the animals, his family and himself. Only when the Ark was finished did God cause rain to fall for forty days and nights, flooding the world.

The biblical tradition of a flood is drawn from earlier sources. There are three Babylonian versions of the story. In one, Xisuthros, the tenth king of Babylon, was told in a dream of the forthcoming disaster by the god Chronus. But unlike Noah, Xisuthros was not permitted to take steps to save himself until he had written a history of the world and buried it at Sippara. Only then was he allowed to start building his own ark.

When the flood waters eventually subsided, Xisuthros went off to explore, leaving his companions in the safety of the ship. After a time, a mysterious voice told them their king was dead ('taken from this world to dwell with the gods') and instructed them to dig up his history at Sippara. They did so and were thus able to rebuild and restore many ancient cities.

The second version of the legend emerges in the famous *Epic of Gilgamesh*. The hero Gilgamesh was born centuries too late to take part in that particular adventure, but his *Epic* tells of Utnapishtim who, like Noah, survived destruction with the help of divine instruction to build an ark. The Utnapishtim version of the story tells of whirlwinds and perpetual darkness, torrential rain and rising waters, but the emergency lasted only a week.

The third, and oldest, version is fragmentary. It appears on a 4,100-year-old clay tablet discovered by archaeologists at Nippur, in Sumer, and tells of King Ziusudra and a priest named Enki surviving the deluge. Unfortunately the tablet was broken, so the story is incomplete.

The patriarch Abraham and his people would have known the legend and carried it with them when they left Chaldea and migrated to Canaan.

In 1929, British archaeologist Leonard Woolley unearthed evidence that the Flood was more than a myth. While excavating the ancient Chaldean city of Ur, he discovered traces of a huge flood which had inundated not only the city, but vast sweeps of the surrounding countryside around 3000 BC. Scholarly opinion seized on the discovery to formulate a theory that the peoples of the ancient Near East had experienced a local flood so extensive they naively imagined it encompassed the whole world.

It is a theory that remains popular to this day, but one that fails to account for the fact that flood legends are universal. The story of the deluge is told in Syria, where the hero is named Sisythes. It appears again in Greece, which has legends of three floods. The best-known story is that of Deucalion and his wife Pyrrha who repopulated the world as the only survivors of a universal flood. But there are two further versions. One tells of a much earlier flood, at the time of Ogyges, King of Thebes, and one of a much later inundation which, while not universal, was severe enough to drive Dardanus from his home to found the city of Troy.

The Hindu *Puranas* give the story of Satyavrata, who escaped a great prehistoric flood with the help of an ark. Iceland's epic poem, the *Edda*, casts the hero Bergelmir and his wife in essentially the same role. There are echoes of an ark in Siberian, Norse and Welsh mythology. It appears again among the native tribes of North and South America, among the Masai of Africa, among the Hottentots, the Australian Aborigines, the Fiji islanders, the Eskimos, the Malays, the Samoans, the Burmese, the Cambodians, the Maoris of New Zealand, the Dyaks of Borneo, and the Chinese.

The Victorian anthropologist, James G. Frazer, claimed that the myths of Africa, northern and central Asia and western Europe contained no flood legends, but then contradicted himself by remarking that there *were* stories of land subsidence and sea inundation. A definitive modern source states categorically that the flood motif is found in 'almost every mythology in the world', the main exceptions being Egypt and Japan.[34]

---

[34] Funk and Wagnalls *Standard Dictionary of Folklore, Mythology and Legend*, Harper, San Francisco, 1984.

Although classified, and dismissed, as mythology, it is clear that most, if not all, of these near-universal legends are distorted memories and interpretations of an actual planetary disaster. Mounting evidence shows the disaster occurred towards the end of the Pleistocene in approximately the same time period that Plato claims saw the disappearance of Atlantis.

Many of the 'myths' contain telling details. In Genesis Chapter 9, the beginnings of agriculture, and in particular the cultivation of the vine, are attributed to Noah, suggesting that farming was not the natural development of a linear evolution, but rather a skill carried over by the survivors of the great disaster. In this context, it is interesting to note that the earliest indications of farming activity worldwide are, almost without exception, found on high ground, exactly what we would expect if we were dealing with a gradually receding flood.

In the religious literature of Mesopotamia, the *Eridu Genesis* is an ancient Sumerian epic primarily concerned with the creation of the world. The work specifically describes the building of cities and the institution of kingship before civilisation was destroyed by a universal flood – essentially the same story told by Plato.

Shuruppak, an ancient Sumerian city located south of Nippur, in what is now south-central Iraq, was celebrated in Sumerian legend as the home of Ziusudra who, like Noah, escaped the deluge by building an ark. Excavations in the first half of the twentieth century unearthed evidence of human habitation extending back to prehistoric times. Among the finds were ruins of well-built houses, along with cuneiform tablets with administrative records and lists of words, indicating a highly developed society in place at an unusually early era. Here too, the theory of rebuilding after devastation would explain how such a culture could spring up apparently fully formed.

A sudden tilting of the Earth's axis would be more than enough to trigger vast tectonic convulsions across the surface of the globe. The same phenomenon might easily have led to the draining of whole seas and the drowning of islands, or even small continents, in floods so extensive as to be nearly universal.

It is relatively easy now to build up a comprehensive picture of the consequences. Whole animal species – mammoths, mastodons, sabre-toothed cats and other giant mammals – were so decimated by the disaster that they never recovered and died out in the bitter aftermath. Humanity survived, but early civilisation did not. Hapgood's mariners, Plato's warlike Atlanteans, the ancient proto-cultures of Athens and Egypt, were all wiped out and evidence of their existence buried so deeply it is only now coming to light in scattered fragments.

In a terrifyingly short period, humanity was hurled back to the Stone Age to begin a long, slow crawl back to cultural levels soon forgotten.

This is the only picture that fits the evidence we have been examining; and it is, not at all coincidentally, the same picture presented by our earliest oral traditions. But it is a picture that remains incomplete. For if prehistoric civilisation was lost in devastating floods, caused by an unimaginable upsurge of world-wide tectonic violence, caused in turn by the sudden tilting of our planetary axis, there is still one question that requires an answer: What caused the Earth to tilt?

Plato attributed the disappearance of Atlantis and the ancient Athenian army to 'extraordinary' earthquakes and floods. But devastating though these must have been to sink an entire island continent, they remain a local phenomenon. They represented no more than the Mediterranean experience of a disaster of planetary proportions and will not help us understand what happened on the broader scale. But there is another reference in Plato's history that may prove more useful.

Plato did not claim direct knowledge of Atlantis. He said he had the story from Critias, who heard it told by the Greek statesman Solon, who in turn had it from a priest of the temple at Sais in Egypt. Before embarking on the story of Atlantis, the priest talked with Solon at some length about world history, largely to make the point that only Egyptian records stretched back to distant antiquity. The reason he gave for this was interesting. There had been, he said, a number of ancient cataclysms so widespread and so violent that they had all but destroyed humanity – completely destroyed mankind's written histories, except in Egypt where a set of unusual circumstances allowed them to be preserved. These ancient histories allowed him to give an unusual interpretation to a popular Greek myth.

In Greek mythology, Phaethon – the name means 'shining' or 'radiant' – was the son of the sun-god Helios, and a mortal woman or nymph. Phaethon was taunted with illegitimacy to such an extent that he appealed to his father for help. Helios swore to prove Phaethon's paternity by giving him anything he would care to ask for. Phaethon promptly demanded to drive the chariot of the sun through the heavens for a single day. Although Helios tried to dissuade him, Phaethon insisted and, bound by his oath, Helios had to let him make the attempt.

Phaethon proved unable to control the horses and the sun chariot came too near the Earth which began to burn up. The flames destroyed nations. The ground burst open and rivers dried up. A pall of smoke brought darkness to the world. The ocean shrank. Ashes covered the Earth. The Earth itself was shifted and asked the help of Jupiter:

> If the sea, if the earth, if the palace of heaven, perish, we are then jumbled into the old chaos again. Save it from the flames, if ought still survives, and preserve the universe.

To prevent further damage, Zeus hurled a thunderbolt at Phaethon, who fell to the Earth at the mouth of the River Eridanus.[35]

Helios promptly went into mourning and hid his face so that the Earth was lit only by its own flames. He refused to resume his daily journey until all the gods paid him homage. When this was duly done, the normal sequence of day and night reappeared. Jupiter restored order and life to the heavens and Earth.

On the face of it, this seems no more than another of those engaging fables for which the ancient Greeks were famous. But the Egyptian priest who spoke with Solon thought otherwise. He claimed it was a mythic description of an actual astronomical event.

---

[35] Which scholars now identify as the River Po in Italy.

14

ASTEROIDS AND COMETS

_____ **FACT** _____

COLLISION WITH A COMET WOULD BE A DREADFUL,

DESTRUCTIVE AND TERRIFYING EVENT, BUT IT

WOULD NOT EQUATE TO THE GLOBAL CATACLYSM

THAT SANK ATLANTIS.

Between 16 July and 22 July 1994, more than twenty fragments of a disintegrating comet – named Shoemaker-Levy 9 after the astronomers who discovered it – crashed into the planet Jupiter. The word *fragments* is deceptive. What struck Jupiter was a series of masses anything up to one mile in diameter and travelling at some 2,200 miles an hour. Each strike produced dramatic results. There were vast explosions, fiery plumes thousands of miles high, huge bubbles of hot gas in the Jovian atmosphere and large dark scars on the observable planetary disc that took weeks to disappear.

Jupiter is a giant planet, 318 times as massive as the Earth and with more than 1,500 times the volume. It was clear to observers who monitored the event, that had Shoemaker-Levy missed Jupiter and struck our own planet, the consequences would have been devastating.

There was, however, some reassurance from the experts at the time. Apart from the sun, Jupiter is the largest body in the solar system. Its massive gravitational field tends to act as a sort of cosmic vacuum cleaner to sweep up debris entering the system from outside. It was no coincidence that Shoemaker-Levy struck Jupiter, which stands like a sentinel protecting the inner planets – including Earth – from harm. Unfortunately, this insurance policy is not fully comprehensive.

On 20 March 1996, the Jet Propulsion Laboratory at Pasadena, California, announced a scientific team had discovered a chain of impact craters in Chad, central Africa, that suggested Earth was once struck by a large, fragmented comet – or possibly a shattered asteroid – similar to Shoemaker-Levy.

The craters were discovered in radar images of the Earth taken from the space shuttle *Endeavour* in April and October 1994. These images showed two new craters beside a known impact site named Aorounga. They varied in size from 7 to 10 miles and were caused by objects close to a mile in diameter. Chains of similarly sized craters have been seen on Callisto, one of the moons of Jupiter.

Scientists estimate the Chad craters date back about 360 million years. If the estimate is correct, they struck at a time when the Earth was undergoing a period of mass extinctions. There is scientific speculation that, although not big enough to have caused the extinctions on their own, the impacts may have been part of a larger cosmic event.

The question of extinctions triggered by the impact of large bodies from space is one that has increasingly concerned scientists in the final decades of the twentieth century. Although there are several dissenting voices, it is now generally accepted in the scientific community that the death of the dinosaurs, 65 million years ago, was triggered by the impact of an asteroid or comet roughly ten times bigger than the one that broke up to form the craters in Chad. The question that concerns astronomers is whether such an impact could happen again.

Eugene (Gene) Shoemaker, whose name is appended to the comet that collided with Jupiter, was killed on 18 July 1997, in a car accident in Alice Springs, Australia, during field research on impact crater geology. His wife and fellow astronomer Carolyn Shoemaker was injured in the same accident.

Shoemaker's ashes now rest on the moon, in a vacuum-sealed capsule carried there by *Lunar Prospector*. Wrapped around the capsule is a piece of brass foil inscribed with lines from *Romeo and Juliet*:

> And, when he shall die,
> Take him and cut him out in little stars,
> And he will make the face of heaven so fine
> That all the world will be in love with night,
> And pay no worship to the garish sun.

Prior to Shoemaker's death, he and his wife were engaged at Flagstaff, Arizona, on the study and discovery of comets. They were particularly interested in tracking any body that might impact on the Earth and worked hard to alert politicians to the dangers of such events. In common with most astronomers, they believed that a major impact was only a matter of time, and contingency plans should be made to meet such an emergency.

There seems little doubt the astronomers are right. On any night of the year, some fifteen meteors appear in the skies above our planet every hour. Several times over the year – during the aptly named meteor showers – this number increases dramatically to anything up to seventy-five.

Few meteors do any damage. Most are pea-sized pieces of rock and ice – debris from comets and other cosmic bodies – that burn up soon after they strike the Earth's atmosphere. But a few are much more dangerous.

On 10 August 1972, the brightest meteor ever recorded was seen in the *daytime* sky over the United States. It moved at an estimated speed of 33,500 miles an hour across Montana, Wyoming and Utah. Fortunately it did no more than graze the upper reaches of the atmosphere, for satellite observation showed it was far from pea-sized. This meteor had a diameter of 100 feet, more than large enough to cause substantial damage had it reached ground level in a populated area.

And meteorites certainly do reach ground level. The largest known was found in 1920 near Grootfontein, Namibia. It weighed more than 60 tons.

But meteorites, even those as big as the monster that fell on Namibia, are not the major worry. It is two other types of cosmic body that give astronomers their darkest nightmares.

One of these is asteroids. They are small planetary bodies of greatly varying size. The largest representatives are Ceres, with a diameter of about 640 miles, and Pallas and Vesta, with diameters of about 340 miles. About 200 asteroids have diameters of more than 60 miles, and thousands of smaller ones exist.

Although most asteroids are confined to a belt between the orbits of Mars and Jupiter, a number pass inside the Martian orbit and hence are classified as 'near Earth'.

In 1932, the German astronomer Karl Wilhelm Reinmuth became the first person to observe a near-Earth asteroid group that actually crossed our planetary orbit. Because of their poor light-reflecting qualities, asteroids are notoriously difficult to track and Reinmuth lost them shortly after his discovery. Despite his best efforts and those of fellow astronomers, they were not rediscovered until 1978 – just two years after US astronomer Eleanor F. Helin spotted a second group which also crossed our orbit.

The finds caused a flurry of interest. Any major astronomical body that crosses the orbit of the Earth is obviously a potential danger. A dedicated study got under way with the result that some 25 such asteroids were discovered by the end of the 1970s. In the next decade, a further 80 turned up, while by the early 1990s the confirmed total had swelled to 154.

Current estimates place the total number of Earth-crossing asteroids of more than half a mile in diameter at a staggering 1,800. More seem to be on their way. Among the near-Earth asteroids are those that form a group called the Amors. Although they do not cross our orbit regularly at present, the gravitational influences they experience change their orbits appreciably. For this reason, some of these more distant asteroids cross Earth's orbit occasionally and are likely to do so in the future with increasing frequency.

Close approaches to the Earth occur. In January 1991, an asteroid with an estimated diameter of 30 feet passed by the Earth within less than half the distance to the moon. All it needs is a collision with one of the larger asteroids to create a terrestrial disaster.

Asteroids are not the only problem. In the past 2,200 years, 810 comets have visited our solar system. But several of them are on orbits that bring them this way more than once, so the total cometary sightings in the period is 1,292.

New comets are being discovered all the time. Among the more recent was one of the most spectacular. Hale-Bopp was first spotted on 23 July 1995 by two independent observers, Alan Hale and Thomas Bopp. It came closest to Earth on 22 March 1997 and made a spectacular display in the night sky until early May.

Hale-Bobb was never a danger to Earth, but astronomers are painfully aware there are no guarantees this will always be the case with visiting comets. A collision with Earth would be a disaster of the first magnitude.

But even a comet would not shift our planetary axis. Although the gaseous heads of certain comets can exceed the size of Jupiter, the solid portion of most of them is no more than a few cubic miles. Collision with a comet would be a dreadful, destructive and terrifying event, but it would not equate to the global cataclysm that sank Atlantis. Even when we look beyond the Earth, there is nothing in our knowledge to explain what happened 11,600 years ago.

15

MISSING PLANET

——————————— **FACT** ———————————

THE ESTIMATED VOLUME OF ROCKY MATTER IN THE

ASTEROID BELT WOULD BUILD A PLANET SLIGHTLY

SMALLER THAN OUR MOON . . . THE EXPLOSION MUST

HAVE BEEN ENORMOUS.

The world's first astronomers were the Sumerians and the Chaldeans, both early Babylonian peoples. Their level of knowledge was impressive. They knew, for example, that the sun occupied the central position of the solar system – a discovery generally credited to Nicolaus Copernicus in 1543. They knew the moon shone by reflected light and lunar eclipses were caused by the Earth's shadow. They were aware of orbital variations in the planets and had discovered what is known as the precession of the equinoxes.

In compiling his star catalogue in 129 BC, the Greek astronomer Hipparchus recorded that the stars shifted systematically from their positions over an extended time period. The keyword here is *systematically*. It meant it was not the stars that were moving, but the Earth. This movement is now known to be a wobble in the Earth's axis describing a long, slow circle. The result of the wobble is that the constellation coinciding with the equinoxes gradually changes over time.

Today, the precession of the equinoxes is a matter of calculation, but its original discovery would require a prolonged period of observation. Just how prolonged can be deduced from the fact that it takes 2,160 years for any given zodiacal sign marking the vernal (spring) equinox to change. The first time this happens is a mystery. By the time astronomers have seen it happen twice or three times, they may be developing a suspicion about what is going on. But to confirm the entire cycle absolutely requires continuous observation – and the keeping of records – over a 25,920-year period.

Hipparchus made no claim to originality in his discovery. He acknowledged it was actually made by Babylonian astronomers. This was confirmed by Professor Herman Hilprecht in the late nineteenth century after analysis of several thousand clay tablets from the temple libraries of Nippur and Sippar, and from the library of Ashurbanipal, the last of the great kings of Assyria, who reigned from 668 to 627 BC.

Ashurbanipal assembled in Nineveh the first systematically collected and catalogued library in the ancient Near East. About 20,000 of its tablets and fragments have been preserved in the British Museum. He had his scribes search out and collect, or copy, texts of every type from temple libraries to be added to a basic collection from Ashur, Calah and Nineveh itself. The majority of these texts were astronomical or mathematical in nature and many were ancient even in Ashurbanipal's day.

As Hilprecht continued his extensive examination of the tablets, he discovered to his surprise that every multiplication and division table in ancient Babylon was based on the number 12,960,000. Why this should be so remained a mystery until Hilprecht, remembering Babylonian fascination with the stars, hit on the idea that the number might have an astronomical aspect. He made the relevant calculations and concluded it could only be related to the precession of the equinoxes.

But the Babylonians in turn drew their astronomical

knowledge from even earlier sources. A Sumerian tablet in the Berlin Museum lists a zodiac with an equinox point in Leo (today it is in Aries), suggesting the zodiac itself must have been drawn up at least as far back as 11,000 BC, a time when Hapgood's prehistoric civilisation and Plato's Atlantis were still flourishing.

In 1955, Professors George Sarton and O. Neugebauer published separate findings on Assyrian, Chaldean and Sumerian astronomical tables showing they were not based on direct observation but on mathematical formulae inherited from an earlier time. There is nothing in the archaeological record to show where these formula were first developed.

The degree of sophistication achieved by the Babylonian astronomers – with the help of inherited knowledge – is underlined by the discovery of a clay tablet from Ur dating back to the third millennium BC. This tablet divides the heavens into three distinct regions, a schematic only adopted by modern astronomers as late as 1925.

Faced with the advances of ancient Near Eastern astronomy, it comes as no surprise to discover the Babylonians knew there were more members of the solar system than those visible to the naked eye.

Today, astronomers recognise the solar system as comprised of the sun and nine planets – Mercury, Venus, Earth, Mars, Jupiter, Saturn, Uranus, Neptune and Pluto. Of these, only Mercury, Venus, Mars and Jupiter can be seen without a telescope. In the State Museum of the former East Berlin is an Akkadian cylinder depicting all nine planets and the moon. But this cylinder – and several others like it – shows a *tenth* planet in the system.

Bode's Law, formulated in the eighteenth century, is a way of calculating the average distance of each planet from the sun.

Although the exact calculation is a little more complicated,[36] this law states that each planet orbits the sun at roughly twice the distance of the previous one. When it was first announced in 1766 by the German astronomer Johann Daniel Titus and popularised by Johann Bode in 1772, only six planets were known and it worked well for five of them. Mercury, Venus, Earth, Mars and Saturn all obeyed the law. Jupiter did not.

Although a useful rule of thumb, the Jupiter hiccup meant Bode's Law received little attention from astronomers until 1781, when William Herschel discovered a seventh planet. He named it Georgium Sidus, in honour of his royal patron King George III, but this was changed to Herschel by the astronomical community, then later renamed Uranus in the classical tradition. Uranus, amazingly, was located exactly where Bode's Law predicted.

Bode's Law failed again for Neptune, discovered in 1846, but accurately predicted the orbit of Pluto, first observed in 1905.

This 'not-quite law' is viewed as an astronomical curio today, but in 1781 it had begun to look so rock-solid that scientists were no longer questioning the 'law' but rather looking for the missing planet it predicted between Mars and Jupiter. Many astronomical searches were organised and some quite substantial prizes offered. None were claimed until New Year's Day 1801, when the Italian astronomer Guiseppe Piazzi finally found what everybody had been looking for.

Piazzi was making routine observations when a planetary body swam into view just where Bode's Law had predicted. But it was the oddest planetary body in the entire solar system. With a diameter of only about 640 miles it was so tiny it was dwarfed by most

---

[36] Take the sequence 0,3,6,12,24,48 and 96. Add four to each number and divide the result by ten. Six of your seven answers – the first five and the last – give you the approximate distance from the sun, in astronomical units, of the six planets known in Bode's day.

known moons and its orbit was quite unlike any other. Piazzi's discovery was named Ceres.

Scientists were still puzzling over this bewildering find when, just over a year later, the German astronomer Heinrich Olbers observed a second body near Ceres. This one was even smaller, but it too orbited the sun just like the other planets. It was named Pallas and its discoverer promptly predicted that many more such bodies would soon be found. He forecast that they would vary in brightness as they spun on their axes, indicating irregular shapes, and that their orbits would be just as peculiar as those of the first two observed.

Olbers proved absolutely right. Subsequent observations showed Ceres and Pallas were just two members of a massive asteroid belt lying between the orbits of Mars and Jupiter. There were literally thousands of rocky masses circling the sun within it. Some 200 had diameters of more than 60 miles. The rest were smaller and many were very much smaller. Although the larger bodies were roughly spherical, like the known planets, irregular shapes were common for those with diameters of less than 100 miles. All seemed to rotate. Some rotated five times faster than the Earth.

Most meteorites recovered on Earth are now believed to be asteroid fragments, except for a very few that have been traced to the moon or Mars – and even these may have been 'splashed off' the surface of these bodies in the course of asteroid/meteorite bombardment.

As more and more discoveries were made in the asteroid belt, a puzzle emerged. A few asteroids seem to have a surface composition like that of lava. This has led astronomers to conclude these bodies were once at least partly melted. The mystery arises because only some were melted. Astronomers are hard put to suggest a mechanism that would lead to this result.

Had he known of the erratic melting, Olbers himself would have been less puzzled. He based his original prediction on a dramatic premise. He believed there had once been a fully formed planet in the orbit forecast by Bode's Law. That planet exploded.

When Olbers first announced his idea, it gained a sympathetic reception from his peers. The concept of an exploded planet seemed like a common-sense explanation of the debris orbiting between Mars and Jupiter.

In 1814, Louis Lagrange, a French astronomer, decided a cosmic explosion might explain the existence of comets as well. He was suspicious of their elongated orbits which he believed meant they must have been thrown out of the solar system with great force. Lagrange provoked the ire of his fellow-countryman and astronomer, the Marquis de Laplace, who leaped to defend his own nebular theory of cometry origins. The prestige of Laplace won the day. A scientific consensus emerged. No planet had exploded. Asteroids and comets had other explanations. Consensus or not, there were dissenting voices.

In 1948, astronomers H. Brown and C. Patterson published a report presenting evidence that meteorites were once part of a planet. Since, as we have already seen, most meteorites are fragments of asteroids, this was essentially the same claim as made by Olbers.

In 1993, American astronomer Tom Van Flandern, a former director of the Celestial Mechanics Branch of the US Naval Observatory, argued the same theory strongly.

In 1972, Canadian astronomer Michael Ovenden developed a law similar to Bode's, but far more precise and complex in its structure. The Ovenden formula not only predicts the placing of the planets, but details their major satellites as well. Like Bode, he concluded there was a planet missing, but went an important step further. His calculations told him the planet must have been a giant, at least the size of Saturn.

The estimated volume of rocky matter in the asteroid belt would build a planet slightly smaller than our moon. If Ovenden is right, several possibilities arise. One is that the original planet was a gas giant with a very tiny rocky core. Another is that, however it was structured, large parts of the missing planet are no longer in our solar system. A third – disturbing – possibility is that a large portion of the planet's original mass must have been converted into energy. That means the explosion must have been enormous.

Current astronomical theory indicates the solar system was formed when the sun itself came into being about 4.7 billion years ago. Astronomers believe it all started with an interstellar cloud of gas and dust and a nearby supernova.

Supernovas are stars that explode so violently they destroy themselves. The amount of energy released is almost unimaginable. It would certainly have influenced any nearby gas clouds with the distinct possibility of fragmentation and gravitational collapse.

One result of the collapse was the formation of a dense central region with enough errant energies and gravitational pressures to trigger the nuclear furnaces of a brand new sun. In essence, our sun 'condensed' out of the gas cloud.

Astronomers believe the other bodies in the solar system condensed as well, and at much the same time. Observation seems to support this theory. The region closest to the new sun would be so hot that it would inhibit the condensation of anything lighter than iron. Mercury, the closest planet to the sun, has an unusually large, dense, iron core. At greater distances, gases condense into solids such as are found in Jupiter and the outer planets.

Orthodox astronomical theory has it that the asteroid belt condensed in its current orbit at the same time as the planets. But the evidence is against it.

If the asteroids were formed at the same time as the sun and planets, they would now be more than 4.5 billion years old. In that time, the predicted rate of collision would make sure there were no sizeable asteroids left – they would all be smashed into tiny fragments. But there are large asteroids left.

Assume that, miraculously, the asteroids have been colliding for billions of years without fragmenting. Those collisions produce another problem. Each time an asteroid collides, its speed relative to the other asteroids reduces.

By now, you would expect very little difference in asteroid speeds, especially since there would not be much of a difference to begin with if they all condensed out of a gas cloud at the same time as the sun. But astronomers have calculated that the average difference in the orbiting speeds of various asteroids is a massive 3 miles a second. This is far too high.

Many of the asteroids that have been closely studied by astronomers turn out to have satellites – little 'moons' – that orbit around them. You can explain the moons of the larger planets easily enough. They arise from gravitational capture or a fragmentation from the parent body. But the dynamics don't work the same way for a collection of smaller objects like the asteroids. You might find a freak satellite or two, but not the numbers currently showing up in the asteroid belt.

As against that, the gravitational dynamics of an exploding planet would produce asteroid satellites as a matter of course. The explosion itself must have occurred recently (in astronomical terms). Give the asteroids anything more than a few million years and gravitational forces and collisions would destroy the satellites.

Those satellites also account for meteor showers. When an asteroid's orbit brings it closest to the sun, there is a tendency for any satellites to break away and go into solar orbit themselves. Conventional astronomers, who believe meteorites arise from asteroid collisions, see no reason why this should happen. But the fact is it does. All four known asteroid-related meteor streams arise when the asteroids are closest to the sun.

Finally, there are still about 1,000 Earth-crossing asteroids bigger than half a mile in diameter. If those asteroids had been around for 4.7 billion years, they would have long since crashed to ground. Astrophysicists calculate that the absolute maximum time they could survive is 30 million years. This means they *can't* have been formed at the same time as the sun.

16

DEVASTATED SOLAR SYSTEM

_____ FACT _____

AS MORE THAN ONE ASTRONOMER HAS OBSERVED,

IF A PLANET EXPLODED, THE EVIDENCE SHOULD BE

SCATTERED ACROSS THE ENTIRE SOLAR SYSTEM. THIS

CERTAINLY SEEMS TO BE THE CASE.

There is further (circumstantial) evidence of a cosmic explosion on various planets and satellites of the solar system.

Mercury rotates slowly. Its day is 57.8 Earth days long. Because of this, any planetary explosion would pepper it with debris on one side only. Observations show one side of Mercury is cratered far more heavily than the other.

Although the atmosphere of Venus is largely comprised of carbon dioxide, there is a cloud base of concentrated sulphuric acid. At 459°C, the surface temperature is high enough to melt lead. Atmospheric pressure is 96 times that of Earth. Conditions like these erode surface features very quickly, yet Venus is heavily cratered with little or no sign of erosion. One explanation might be that the planet was bombarded from space in relatively recent times.

Although surface conditions are nowhere near so extreme as Venus, the frequent sandstorms on Mars have much the same eroding effect. Yet the Red Planet too is heavily cratered.

Water is extremely rare on Venus, even in the form of vapour. Yet an abundance of heavy hydrogen, which forms from water, indicates there must have been oceans on the planet at one time. Astronomers find it difficult to believe that oceans formed naturally on the planet, leading to the possibility that there was a massive 'dumping' of water on Venus at the time of a planetary explosion.

That there may have been a great deal of water on the exploded planet is attested to by the fact that its assumed remnants – asteroids and comets – are about one-fifth water by bulk.

The dumping would not have been confined to Venus, of course. In this context, there are indications of water – in the form of ice – on the moon. This is an impossibility unless it arrived from space.

Tektites are small, glassy objects that have presented something of a mystery to geologists. They are found scattered in their millions in an S-shaped belt over a large area stretching from Australia, through south-eastern Asia, eastern Europe, the western coast of Africa, South America, all the way to Texas. Since they differ from the rock groups in which they are found, the consensus among scientists is that they originated outside the planet. Current theories include the possibility that tektites are lunar material splashed off in meteorite collisions or that they were formed by a meteorite collision on Earth hurling large amounts of debris into the atmosphere.

But the tektites show signs of having been melted *before* they entered the Earth's atmosphere, as well as some re-melting afterwards. The idea of an exploded planet provides a neat explanation of this phenomenon.

Mars has two small moons, Phobos and Diemos. Both are almost certainly captured asteroids. But celestial mechanics make it almost impossible that they should have been captured from a static asteroid belt, while no such difficulty arises if the belt itself resulted from a planetary explosion.

Both Saturn and Uranus are known to have rings. In the case of Saturn, which has been more fully investigated, this spectacular phenomenon starts about 7,000 miles above its equator and extends about 35,000 miles into space. Although the diameter of the system is about 170,000 miles, it is no more than 10 miles thick. The rings of Saturn, and most likely Uranus, are made up of chunks of matter averaging a cubic yard in volume. A process known as gravitational screen capture would neatly account for these rings and the satellites of Jupiter, Saturn, Uranus and Neptune . . . provided an exploding planet sent debris streaming past them. As more than one astronomer has observed, if a planet exploded, the evidence should be scattered across the entire solar system. This certainly seems to be the case.

Slow-rotating satellites show heavy cratering on one side when compared with the other. The effect lessens, as expected, the further you travel from the point of the explosion, but is very clearly discernible on the moon.

Many meteorites – not just tektites – appear to have been subjected to great heat *before* they entered the Earth's atmosphere. Some of them contain diamonds, which form only under the pressures and temperatures found in much larger bodies.

The orbits of comets have a statistical tendency to originate at a common point between Mars and Jupiter, just where the missing planet is supposed to have been. The evidence goes on and on.

Computers can reverse time. If you feed in celestial data and the mathematical formulae governing gravitational influence, orbital velocity and various miscellaneous factors, then run the program backwards, you can see where things came from just as easily as you can predict where they might be going.

The data relating to an extra planet – in particular those cometary orbits – shows it must have exploded some 3.2 million years ago. That's far too long to account for the terrestrial disaster that sank Atlantis.

All the same, there are problems with that dating. The first is the GIGO computer principle – Garbage In, Garbage Out – a picturesque way of emphasising that incorrect data fed into a computer will always result in a wrong answer, however careful the calculation.

The data that leads to the 3.2 million-year dating of the planetary explosion is based almost entirely on assumptions about the origination and age of comets. Whatever their origination – and orthodox astronomy insists they arise in the Oort Cloud, an area of space located some 1,000 times the distance of Pluto from the sun – the age of comets is a matter of very considerable controversy. Speculation literally ranges from 10,000 to 10 million years – a discrepancy that could obviously make nonsense of the planetary explosion calculation. But this is not the only problem.

Mars is Earth's next-door neighbour as you travel outwards from the sun, so the missing planet between Mars and Jupiter is, in astronomical terms, quite close. A massive explosion in that area of space would have had a profound effect on this world.

You might reasonably expect a heavy meteorite bombardment with lots of cratering, a planetary upsurge in volcanic activity, species extinctions, ocean changes, worldwide forest fires, floods and other signs of cosmic violence – signs very similar, in fact, to the events we examined earlier.

Nothing of this sort appears in the Earth's geological record of 3.2 million years ago. Besides, if the planet exploded at that time, how come the Babylonians knew about it?

But if the calculations are in error, even an exploding planet would not account for all that happened to the Earth at the end of the Pleistocene. No amount of meteorite bombardment would shift the axis of our world.

Although the fact is seldom published, there are clear astronomical indications that we live in a violently disrupted solar system. These signs go far beyond the minor inconvenience of an exploded planet.

If one could look down on the solar system from far above the North Pole, the planets would appear to move around the sun in a counter-clockwise direction. But there the uniformity ends.

We have already noted that our own planetary orbit varies from the circle predicted by Newtonian mechanics. Every other planet in the solar system also varies to some degree. Those which come closest to circular orbits are Venus and Neptune where the variation is so small as to be almost negligible.

Earth has twice the variation of these planets. Jupiter and Uranus have five times the variation. Saturn has six, Mars nine, while both Mercury and Pluto, at opposite ends of the system, show more than twenty times the deviation that Venus and Neptune display. Pluto's orbit is so elliptical that it is sometimes closer than Neptune to the sun. Seven of the nine planets rotate in one direction. Two – Venus and Pluto – spin the other way. The entire system is remarkably flat. But Mercury and Pluto have obviously inclined orbits.

Venus rotates too slowly for its size. So does Mars. Earth, on the other hand, rotates a little too quickly. There are indications that it should have – and used to have – a 30-hour day. Interestingly, the extra hours of sunlight added to an upright axis would produce even more idyllic weather and abundant plant growth in the speculative prehistoric Golden Age.

Earth is not the only planet to spin too fast. Jupiter, Saturn, Uranus and Neptune all rotate too quickly for their planetary mass.

Something moved our moon. It once circled the Earth more closely than it does today. Natural orbital decay, which might be expected over many millions of years, would tend to draw it closer, not send it further away.

The Martian moons, Phobos and Diemos, orbit their planet at astonishingly high speed. Diemos takes little more than a day – just over 30 hours – to complete an orbit. Phobos hurtles around in an even more amazing 7 hours and 39 minutes.

Jupiter's two outmost moons orbit from pole to pole, unlike any other satellite in the system, and travel in opposite directions to one another. Jupiter, moreover, has trapped two clusters of asteroids which lead and follow it in its orbit around the sun.

Saturn has a moon that orbits in a retrograde direction – that is, clockwise instead of counter-clockwise. Although its rings may well be small rock fragments, most of its satellites seem to be composed mainly of ice.

Uranus is not only dramatically inclined in its axis of rotation, but has a massive 60° disparity in its magnetic axis. A number of its moons are also tilted and show signs of extreme violence in their geology. Between Saturn and Uranus there is a massive body, discovered in 1977, named Chiron. It follows an eccentric orbit that takes it close to both planets and has a solar year 51 years longer than that of Earth. This monster is up to 200 miles in diameter and may be a major moon somehow ripped from one or other of the two nearby planets.

Neptune has two major moons, Triton and Nereid, both in retrograde orbits and one so elongated that it takes more than an

Earth year to complete a single revolution round the planet. The remaining six moons range from 36 to 258 miles in diameter. All are irregularly shaped and have very dark surfaces.

There are two major asteroid groups – the Apollo and the Amor – which orbit obliquely through the main asteroid belt, as if pulled out of it by some huge gravitational force, or thrown out by a colliding body.

Even without a missing planet, all this adds up to a dramatic picture of major aberrations which, if they occurred together, point to a catastrophe of almost unimaginable magnitude. And more evidence is being collected all the time.

In 1964, NASA launched *Mariner IV*, the first successful mission to Mars. The unmanned probe sent back the first photograph of the planet, from within 6,200 miles of its surface. The images indicated that there were aligned stress fractures along the planetary crust. Something seemed to have damaged the planet, and damaged it badly. These were not meteorite strikes or any common astronomical phenomenon – something fundamental had happened. The question was: What?

As more information was gathered, it became apparent that something had reduced the Martian magnetic field and slowed its rate of rotation by a factor of three – from 8 hours to the present 24 hours 37 minutes. Mars's orbit also seemed to have been disturbed.

There was no easy answer to the questions arising from these observations. The stress fractures had obviously resulted from changes in the planet's equilibrium. Its tiny moons were far too small to have any real effect and the only other influence – that of the sun – was minuscule as well.

One theory put forward was that Mars had once had a massive satellite – something with a diameter in excess of 600 miles – and somehow lost it. What would cause the loss of such a moon was difficult to guess, as was the fact that no such displaced moon has been found anywhere in the solar system.

The evidence of massive changes in our solar system has not, of course, gone unnoticed by astronomers. But since catastrophes have been unfashionable within the scientific community since Victorian times, the consensus is that the changes came about gradually, a little at a time, or, at worse, one at a time.

This consensus is no more than an assumption – and one, moreover, that does not withstand close scrutiny. Many, if not most, of the factors we have just examined could not have come about gradually. Some, like the tilting of whole planets, require such titanic forces to accomplish it that they could not have happened in isolation.

But if all or most of the changes were the result of some gigantic cataclysm, it is reasonable to ask what in the heavens might have caused it.

17

SUPERNOVA FRAGMENT

_____ FACT _____

ALTHOUGH ONLY FOUR SUPERNOVAS HAVE BEEN

POSITIVELY IDENTIFIED IN RECORDED HISTORY . . .

THESE GIGANTIC STELLAR EXPLOSIONS ACTUALLY

OCCUR IN OUR GALAXY AT THE RATE OF ONE EVERY 30

YEARS OR SO. ONE SUCH WAS THE VELA SUPERNOVA.

There are only three things that can cause a planet to explode. One is nuclear fusion. The possibility of naturally occurring nuclear fusion on a planet was extremely controversial until fusion was observed in certain rare geological processes on Earth. It is possible, if unlikely, that such processes could get out of hand, with a resultant explosion. But it is not possible – so the experts claim – for this to happen on a planet of the size predicted by Michael Ovenden for the orbit between Mars and Jupiter.

The second thing that can cause a planet to explode is a matter–antimatter combination. Antimatter is a substance made up of sub-atomic particles that have the same mass as normal particles but an opposite property such as electrical charge or magnetic moment. Its existence was first proposed by Dr Edward Teller, following on the anti-particle theories of British physicist Paul Dirac. A range of anti-particles was finally confirmed in 1955, indicating that antimatter itself must be a reality.

Because of the 'mirror-image' nature of antimatter, any meeting between matter and antimatter results in mutual (and total) annihilation. The energy release is enormous, so impact with something as small as an antimatter meteorite or comet might be enough to detonate a planet.

Unfortunately for the theory that a matter–antimatter explosion destroyed the giant planet that once orbited between Mars and Jupiter, there is a remarkable – and so far unexplained – scarcity of antimatter in the universe. While antimatter meteorites or comets are theoretically possible, there is nothing to suggest they occur in the real world. If antimatter did indeed destroy the missing planet, its only really likely source is manufacture . . . and this presupposes intelligence.

The scenario is fascinating. An intelligent life-form on the now-missing planet evolved sufficiently to develop an antimatter technology. But an experiment got out of control, the magnetic barriers between matter and antimatter broke down, and the resultant explosion destroyed the planet.

The scenario is also unlikely. If Ovenden's calculations are correct, the missing planet was almost certainly a gas giant – not the best candidate for evolving life.

The third thing that can cause a planet to explode is close contact, or collision, with a body substantially larger than itself.

A meteorite – or even a meteorite shower – will not destroy a planet or shift its axis. Neither will a comet. These things are simply too small to generate the necessary energy. The same objection applies to a rogue moon, although collision damage would be horrendous.

To create the sort of effects we have seen within our solar system – the exploded planet, the shifts in axes, the disturbed orbits – you would need not merely something substantially larger than our planet, but something substantially larger than the largest planet affected. This means something at least comparable in size to Jupiter, and quite possibly much bigger.

There is really only one known cosmic body that fits the bill – a massive fragment of an exploding star.

Since humanity first began a systematic study of the heavens, astronomers have frequently noted the appearance of what seemed to be new stars. The word *nova* (which itself means 'new') was coined to describe them.

But as understanding grew, a realisation dawned that the term was in error. The so-called 'new stars' were not new at all. They were simply stars that had been too dim to be seen, but suddenly brightened. Ironically, novas are now believed to be old stars with an excess of helium build-up in their outer layers. This creates a degree of expansion that is simply too rapid to be contained. When it happens, the nova flares to several thousand times its original brightness in a matter of days or even hours. The cause of the brightness is an explosive emission of gas.

About a dozen or so stars go nova in our galaxy each year. The process is locally destructive – life on any orbiting planet would be extremely unlikely to survive – but would not normally be expected to extend much beyond the star's own system. Supernovas are something else.

A supernova explosion is far more spectacular and destructive than a nova. Where novas increase their brilliance by a factor of thousands, supernovas become literally billions of times brighter.

Astronomers are not quite sure why supernovas explode, except in the case of massive stars where the pressure created by core nuclear processes is not enough to withstand the weight of the outer layers. A gravitational collapse occurs and the star blows up. Unlike a nova, this explosion is typically more or less total, sending debris in all directions and often leaving little more than a gaseous shell. The Crab Nebula, one of the many beauties of astronomical observation, is the result of a supernova explosion in AD 1054.

Although only four supernovas have been positively identified in recorded history – the most recent spotted on 24 February 1987 – these gigantic stellar explosions actually occur in our galaxy at the rate of one every 30 years or so. One such was the Vela supernova. In astronomical terms it was located fairly close to our solar system – a mere 45 light years away. According to best estimates, it exploded between 14,000 and 11,000 years ago.

Taking this gigantic stellar explosion as our starting point, it becomes possible to build up a picture of what may have happened to our solar system, to our planet and, finally, to Plato's lost Atlantis. What follows is obviously speculation, but speculation based on a wealth of circumstantial evidence.

Towards the end of the Pleistocene era on Earth, a star exploded in the constellation Vela. Enormous fiery fragments were hurtled into space, leaving only a swiftly spinning neutron pulsar that can still be observed by astronomers to this day . . .

One such fragment, larger than the largest planet known, hurtled in the direction of our solar system, a blazing miniature sun with awesome destructive potential. Propelled by the energy of the gigantic explosion, it was likely to achieve a measurable fraction of the speed of light. Even so, it would have taken more than a century – perhaps several centuries – to reach the orbits of our outermost planets.

The solar system it approached was very different from the solar system as it is today. Planetary orbits were, without exception, closer to the perfect circle predicted both by our God-fearing ancestors and the basic laws of celestial mechanics.

There was almost certainly an extra planet – a gas giant 90 times the mass of our own – orbiting at 2.79 times the distance of Earth from the sun between the orbits of Mars and Jupiter. There may have been yet another in the outer reaches of the solar system beyond the orbit of Pluto.

The evidence for an eleventh planet is difficult to assess because of the distances involved, but Californian and Hawaiian observatories have now confirmed the existence of the Kuiper Belt first proposed by the Dutch-born American astronomer Gerald Kuiper in 1951.

The Kuiper Belt, like the Oort Cloud, is a region of space believed to contain comets. While the Oort Cloud is spherical, the Kuiper Belt is flattened and much nearer to the sun – so much nearer, in fact, that it might reasonably be considered a part of the solar system. Observations have now shown it is composed of many thousands of orbiting objects, but since their composition is not yet known, it is impossible to say whether they are rocky fragments or chunks of ice. What is known is that not all the objects are small. Two have been discovered with a diameter of 150 miles, their orbits intersecting that of Pluto.

In all this, the Kuiper Belt appears to be at least superficially similar to the asteroid belt. If the asteroid belt is the remains of an exploded planet, there is a possibility that the Kuiper Belt might be too.

Pluto itself may well have been in a wholly different place as the supernova fragment approached. Pluto's origins are frankly mysterious. It differs significantly from the outer planets in just about all its physical properties and with a diameter of approximately 1,430 miles, it is only about two-thirds the size of the moon.

Since many of its properties are similar to those of Triton, the largest of Neptune's known satellites, several astronomers have proposed that what is now our outmost planet may once have been a moon forming part of the Neptunian system.

Thus we return to a picture of a ten-planet solar system. Our central sun was orbited by Mercury, Venus, Earth, Mars, Planet X (now the asteroid belt), Jupiter, Saturn, Uranus, Neptune (with Pluto as one of its satellites) and Planet Y (where the Kuiper Belt is now located).

If the Kuiper Belt, like the asteroid belt, represents the remnants of an outer planet, then that body was the first victim of the Vela intruder. A close pass or direct collision caused the planet to explode in a flash of light that must, momentarily, have rivalled the sun.

Evidence of this vast detonation is not confined to orbiting boulders. Astronomers have detected an Aluminium-26 cloud in the vicinity similar to those generated in supernova explosions. An actual supernova explosion so close to Earth would have destroyed our planet and the rest of the solar system with it, so we are thrown back on the possibility that only a supernova fragment was involved.

Fragment or not, the Vela intruder was massive enough to emerge from the cosmic explosion virtually unscathed. It continued its breakneck penetration of the solar system, but may have been diverted from its original trajectory by the massive gravitational field of Neptune. The pass was close enough to generate intense electrical discharges as field forces around both bodies began to interact. Neptune's two moons, Triton and Nereid, were violently disrupted and Pluto ripped from the system to be flung into a new orbit around the sun.

Voyager 2 observations revealed that Neptune is circled by at least four rings, composed mainly of tiny particles. In the outer ring the particles have an uneven distribution, clumping in five distinct zones. This ring phenomenon is so difficult to explain by natural processes that one is tempted to speculate it too came into being as a result of the Vela interaction, which may also explain why Neptune's magnetic field is so much less than those of the other planets.

It is highly unlikely that there was any direct collision between the Vela fragment and Neptune, otherwise the damage would certainly have been much worse than it was. But the immense mass of the Vela intruder generated such a gravitational field that the outer planet was tilted some 29° on its axis of rotation.

Had it not been for this close encounter with Neptune, there is the barest possibility that the Vela fragment might have done no more than graze the outer reaches of our system. But while smaller than the intruder, Neptune remains a giant planet, 17 times more massive than the Earth and with 44 times its volume.

Its gravitational attraction tugged the Vela fragment inwards and sent it hurtling towards Uranus.

Uranus is almost 15 times as massive as the Earth and has more than 50 times its volume. The Vela intruder, now weakened by collision with one planet and a gravitational tussle with another, began to show its own small degree of disintegration. Four pieces, each as large as a major asteroid, broke off to fly with the intruder or possibly take up orbit around Uranus as moons.

The planet itself now has 15 known satellites. The largest of them, Miranda, Umbriel, Ariel, Oberon and Titania, have diameters ranging from 293 to 980 miles. Oddly, the gravitational fields of two of the smaller moons hold in place one of the ten rings now known to orbit Uranus.

All of the rings consist of boulders about 3 feet in diameter. Their composition is not known for certain, but they are probably rock fragments and water ice mixed with a black polymer. The gaps between the rings are filled with bright dust particles. It may be that the rings are a fragmented satellite of the planet, or even pieces of the Vela intruder itself.

The intruder seems to have speeded the rotation of the planet and also knocked it on its side. Uranus is surrounded by a magnetic field like that of the Earth, but unlike Earth, the axis of this field is tilted 58.6° from the planet's axis of rotation. The Earth's field, by comparison, is tilted a mere 11°. The axis of Uranus's rotation now lies in the plane of its orbit, so that the planet is literally spinning on its side. Other planets have shown a displacement from the vertical, but none anything like as extreme as this.

Leaving the badly displaced Uranus, the Vela intruder hurtled onwards to the planet Saturn.

The Roche Limit, named after French astronomer Édouard Roche who first calculated it, represents the minimum distance one astronomical body can approach another without the smaller being torn apart by tidal forces. It is not relevant to small objects, which means that things like meteors can reach Earth without disintegration. But if you have two massive objects of similar composition, like a planet and its moon, then the Roche Limit of approach is roughly 2.5 times the radius of the larger.

The rings of Saturn lie within the planetary Roche Limit. It may be that they are not captured fragments of an exploded planet after all.

Perhaps the pass of the Vela intruder to the planet Saturn was close enough to fragment a moon – or moons – to create the planet's spectacular rings. The physics of the situation indicate it is entirely possible. But if so, the intruder did not stop with one spectacular effect. It also speeded up Saturn's rotation and pushed the moon Phoebe into a retro orbit.

In 1977, the American astronomer Charles Kowal discovered what he believed to be the most distant minor planet. Named Chiron, it follows an unstable, eccentric orbit between Saturn and Uranus.

Although reclassified as a comet in 1989, because it was surrounded by a cloud of particles, this 250-mile diameter body may actually have been another of Saturn's moons, ripped from its orbit by the Vela fragment and sent to circle the sun as had happened earlier with Pluto. The Vela intruder continued to plunge towards the centre of the solar system.

Jupiter remained largely unaffected, possibly on account of its great size, but more likely because it had attained a position in its solar orbit that kept it clear of the intruder. Thus the next encounter was with Planet X, the gas giant in orbit between Jupiter and Mars.

This encounter may have been an actual collision for the planet exploded, hurling a bombardment of debris at its nearest neighbours and beyond. Several massive fragments were captured in the gravitational field of the Vela intruder and carried along with it towards Mars.

The Red Planet is a desolate wasteland today, but there are

clear signs it once had open water and NASA claims there was a time it harboured life. There is controversial evidence that this life may have evolved intelligence sufficiently high to create an advanced civilisation.[37] If so, it is tempting to speculate whether that civilisation ended – with Martian life itself – under the devastating impact of a close call from the Vela intruder.

Whatever happened, it seems the intruder did slow the axial rotation of Mars, causing such stresses that the Martian crust fractured and split. One or more of the intruder's accompanying fragments may have been captured to provide Mars with Phobos and Diemos, its two peculiar moons.

With a trail of devastation in its wake, the Vela intruder now hurtled towards Earth.

---

[37] See my *Martian Genesis*, Piatkus Books, London, 1998.

18

WAR IN HEAVEN

FACT

IN THE COURSE OF A FEW SHORT DAYS, THE
PEACEFUL WORLD WAS TRANSFORMED INTO A
SCREAMING CHAOS OF TEMPEST, DARKNESS,
HEAT, EARTHQUAKE AND FLOOD.

Like the solar system as a whole, the Earth was very different from the way it is today as disaster raced towards it from the sky.

A near upright axis of rotation combined with a more circular orbit and slower rate of spin to generate an idyllic environment. Days were long and balmy, seasonal variations almost non-existent. Tectonic activity was muted and, in any case, confined to a few clearly defined danger zones. Hurricanes, typhoons and tornadoes were virtually unknown. Even rain was rare – luxuriant vegetation was watered by the morning mists.

The Earth was an old, sedate and comfortable planet. Its geological processes were gradual – the slow erosion of low mountain chains, themselves scarcely more than hills, the unhurried tidal influences of ancient seas.

The fauna of this gentle planet was abundant. Great herds of herbivores roamed its broad plains. The lush vegetation supported many giant species – mammoth, mastodon, cave lion, sloth – known today only from their fossil bones.

Humanity was well established, widespread and civilised. The histories record an Atlantic archipelago with at least one island large enough to be considered a small continent. Worldwide trade links had been established, reaching as far as China and an ice-free Antarctica. Technology, while differently based from that of today, had reached some surprising peaks, notably in the fields of engineering, architecture, optics, astronomy, navigation, cartography and, perhaps (static) electricity.

It was no longer a particularly peaceful society. There were colonies in Europe, north Africa and North and South America which one might guess had not been established without blood-shed. There was certainly a conflict of interest between the Atlantean culture and various advanced Mediterranean states. Warfare itself was in its infancy – the first major conflict had broken out only within recent history – but humanity was learning fast.

The experiment with war, in all probability, was not welcomed by philosophers who may have warned that humanity's offence to its gods would attract a dire judgement. Soon it must have seemed their warnings were all too accurate.

2

The planets of our solar system, with the sole exception of Earth, are named for ancient deities: Mercury, the cosmic messenger, Venus the goddess of love, Mars the god of war, and so on through to Pluto, the dark god of the Underworld.

In this, modern astronomy follows a custom established by cultures like those of ancient Egypt and Sumer. But while today few scientists believe the planets to be actual gods, the ancient peoples of the world seem to have been united in considering them just that. The literal nature of this concept is difficult for us to grasp. The modern separation of religion and science relegates the former to the realm of symbols and leaves all practical application to the latter. It was not so in ancient times. The priest-scientists who looked for insights into the nature and actions of their gods found them in a careful study of the heavens. Where they differed from modern astronomers was not in their observation but in their interpretation.

Today, the fall of a meteorite or the movement of a planet is seen as a meaningless event governed by purely mechanical laws. In Mesopotamia or Egypt, the same observation would have been seen as the dance of a deity.

As the Vela fragment entered our solar system and began its destructive passage, humanity everywhere must have accepted without hesitation that it was witnessing a war in heaven.

The first intimation of anything amiss may have been a deep-space observation of the intruder itself. As a supernova fragment, the body could well have retained its nuclear fires and thus would present itself as a miniature travelling star that shone like the sun with its own light.

Although scientists now assume our distant ancestors could not have developed optical aids to their astronomical interests, historical records clearly show they were aware of planets and satellites invisible to the naked eye. Their observational skills were, in all probability, well able to spot the approaching intruder. But even if not, the astronomers of ancient Athens and Atlantis could not have failed to notice the explosion that produced the Kuiper Belt. At that point, without doubt, a new star appeared in the heavens – and that meant a new god.

It is easy to see how the observed approach of the Vela

fragment could have given rise to the Greek myth of Phaethon. Here was a fiery body that suddenly appeared in the sky. Its radiant nature suggested it might be a son of the sun, but its sudden appearance suggested illegitimacy. The phenomenon was understood as the action and interaction of deities.

The Vela fragment must have seemed a wrathful god. Having announced his presence with an orgy of destruction, this fiery deity approached the great god Neptune, guardian of the deep. Today, Neptune is most often associated with the sea, but in classical times and earlier, his depths were the depths of space. The encounter went badly for those who venerated Neptune. The intruder stole one of his greatest treasures – the companion body now known as Pluto – and hurled it away.

After approaching Uranus and slaughtering one or more of his companions, the new god stole a moon from Saturn and threw it too into the deep.

But these were just preliminaries, a mischievous dance, compared with what happened next. For the newcomer fought with the god whose station in the heavens was between that of Mars and Jupiter, and destroyed him utterly. This must have been a moment of deep terror for the ancient priest-astronomers. If there truly was an extra planet on the outer reaches of the solar system, it could have been beyond even their skills of observation. Or, if they knew about it, it may have appeared so faint and distant as to seem unimportant.

But the giant planet between Mars and Jupiter was quite another story. With a mass now estimated at 90 times that of the Earth,[38] it would have been a dominant feature of the night sky, a god of great stature and importance. The gods were, of course, immortal – a philosophical concept borne out by generations of observations. No one in the whole of recorded history had

[38] By astronomer Tom Van Flandern.

ever witnessed a god die. Yet the fiery interloper slew this one following a battle that may have lasted no more than a few short hours or days.

With the giant planet destroyed, the priests must have watched in horror as the interloper, now joined by several companions – enormous pieces of the shattered planet caught up in the intruder's gravitational field – raced beyond the orbit of Mars in its approach to Earth.

If the Atlantean–Athenian conflict was truly the first great war humanity experienced, then this mind-numbing war in heaven must have seemed connected. Had humankind taught bad habits to the gods? If so, an unimaginable retribution was obviously on its way. Once again the priest-astronomers were absolutely right.

Various forces are involved when one large astronomical body approaches too close to another. One is gravitational, another electrical, or, more properly, electro-magnetic. In the case we have been examining, another factor may have been simple heat exchange. It is entirely possible the Vela fragment was burning like a sun.

It is fairly clear that the intruder must eventually have come so close to Earth that it actually passed within the orbit of the moon. This is the only approach that would permit it to force the moon into a wider orbit. But long before that happened, Vela-F (as we can now call it for convenience) would have come to dominate the night sky, then to appear in daylight as it approached closer and closer.

The gravitational effects are the most likely to have been experienced first. These were fourfold. The strong gravitational field of the intruder and its new companions would:

▲ Disturb the Earth's ancient orbit

▲ Cause the planetary axis to tilt

▲ Slow the speed of rotation

▲ Create the pronounced wobble we now experience in the precession of the equinoxes.

Although the most dramatic in actual terms, the first of these would have produced fewest problems for life on Earth. The change in orbit would have been most evident in the position and appearance of the sun, with some corresponding differences in stellar and planetary observations. But while meaningful to priest-astronomers, it is doubtful if the common mass of humanity would have paid much attention to the change. The remaining effects would have seen to it that they had much more immediate things to worry about.

The Earth consists of three parts, a lithosphere, mantle and core. The lithosphere is a rocky crust that extends to depths of 60 miles. The mantle and core are the heavy interior of the planet, making up most of its mass.

The lithosphere is made up of two shells, known as the crust and the upper mantle. The upper mantle is separated from the lower mantle below by a zone called the asthenosphere, a 60-mile thickness of molten rock.

Heat from the Earth's inner core is continually radiated outward. Convection currents within the mantle transfer most of it to the surface via a worldwide system of mid-ocean ridges. These currents also carry the lava that erupts from volcanoes on land.

In normal times, the system is sedate. Even the most powerful volcanic explosion is of little significance when seen in context with the planet as a whole. But a sudden tilting of the Earth, or a sudden change in its rate of rotation, would have placed almost unimaginable strains on the lithosphere with predictable results.

As the gravitational influence of Vela-F took hold, the shell of our planet began to crack. The fractures were enormous. One remains visible today in the Great Rift Valley, Africa, a fissure that extends more than 3,000 miles from Syria to Mozambique. The width of the valley ranges from a few miles to more than 100.

The splitting of the Earth's crust was accompanied by dramatic changes in its molten interior. The age-old heat circulation system broke down completely as magma flows beneath the surface were drawn increasingly towards the intruder, exactly as ocean tides result from the gravitational pull of the moon.

Nor was the liquid asthenosphere the only thing to be affected. Even the rocky crust of the lithosphere was not immune to that fatal attraction. Already stressed by the cracks and fractures occasioned by planetary tilt, vast reaches of the lithosphere began to buckle and collapse. The great mountain ranges of our present world were folded up to greet the new god in the sky.

There was volcanic activity on a scale never witnessed before. Today there are an estimated 1,300 active volcanoes worldwide. Then, rivers of lava oozed from hundreds of thousands of new cracks. Volcanoes erupted with unparalleled violence. Millions of tons of hot ash were hurled into the atmosphere. As the fiery Vela-F approached, radiation from this secondary sun began to raise the planetary temperature.

But this was not all the tortured Earth had to endure. The change in planetary rotation triggered windstorms of inexpressible violence. These global tornadoes were quite capable of flattening whole forests and whipping tons of dust and debris into the atmosphere to join the volcanic ash already there. The world descended into a howling nightmare of increasing darkness, illuminated only by the dread volcanic fires.

As vast areas of the planet's crust subducted, the rivers, lakes, seas and oceans of the world began to change their courses, draining hugely into the newly created valleys, hollows and lowlands.

The terror engendered in humanity by this sudden chaos can be readily imagined. In the course of a few short days, the peaceful world was transformed into a screaming chaos of tempest, darkness, heat, earthquake and flood. Stone buildings collapsed like matchstick models. Fresh water was polluted and supplies dried up. The ground swelled and buckled beneath the feet. Choking volcanic gas was vented everywhere. An ash-laden darkness was impenetrable by torchlight. There was noise everywhere, day and night.

As Vela-F drew closer still, a new and terrifying phenomenon occurred. Field forces generated by Earth and the approaching intruder sought balanced potential in the exchange of vast electrical lightning bolts. From the viewpoint of our ancestors, this was the beginning of a global thunderstorm beyond their experience. Here, perhaps, was born the tradition of the Jovian thunderbolt – murderous discharges that shook the ground with their violence.

So it went on, chaos upon chaos. No longer able to survive in their old habitats, people left their ruined cities to take refuge in caves and anywhere else that offered even a semblance of safety. Some walled themselves in, hoping to escape the lightning and the storms. And still Vela-F approached.

There was no direct collision, otherwise Earth would not have survived. A portion of a supernova capable of destroying a giant planet beyond the orbit of Mars would have had little difficulty in fragmenting our own. Like Phaethon and his chariot, the burning mass of Vela-F came close, in astronomical terms, to grazing the tortured Earth, then swept onwards towards Venus and the sun. But one or more of its accompanying fragments, torn from the body of the exploded planet beyond Mars, encroached on the Roche Limit and themselves exploded. The great meteor bombardment of the Earth began.

19

COSMIC
BOMBARDMENT

————————— F A C T —————————

BUT THOSE WHO WATCHED TERRIFIED AS THE DISASTER

UNFOLDED WOULD NOT NECESSARILY HAVE

INTERPRETED IT IN THE TERMS WE WOULD USE TODAY.

AS GIANT METEORS RAINED DOWN, THEY COULD

EASILY HAVE CONCLUDED THAT VELA-F ITSELF WAS

BEING HURLED TO EARTH . . .

The myths of many races speak vividly of this bombardment, just as they speak vividly of the days of darkness, the constant earthquakes and the howling storms before it began.

About 2,000 Indians of Algonquin ancestry live in present-day Canada, mainly in Ontario and Québec. Their preserved traditions recall a time in deep prehistory when the brothers Chakekenapok and Manibozho fought a vicious battle in the sky. Manibozho won and broke Chakekenapok into several thousand pieces which rained down on the land. Interestingly, the Algonquins say an extraordinary tornado was devastating the world as the battle was fought. Their tradition also claims that the boulders and rocks sometimes found in isolation on the prairies – those that would now be called glacial erratics – were stones thrown during the celestial combat.

In Central America, a Mexican legend tells how fire and red-hot stones (meteorites) rained down in such numbers that they flattened whole forests. The Toltecs have the same tradition embodied in a prehistoric rain of fire and stones. A Peruvian myth echoes the event in a story of a 'great stone' which fell from heaven to shatter into 1,600 pieces.

Ancient Chinese histories insist there was a time when a planet (or planets) approached close to the Earth, causing vast showers of stones. In Africa, legend states an evil people in the Atlas mountains were punished by a rain of stones from heaven.

There are legends of massive bombardment from the sky by stones or fiery objects in the traditions of Britain, Finland, Greece, Iceland, Scandinavia, Babylonia, Assyria, Indonesia, Palestine, New Zealand and Samoa. The same story is told by the Druids, the Copts, the Hebrews, the Muslims, the Zunis of New Mexico, and the Maya of Guatemala. But the reality of this vast cosmic bombardment does not rely on mythic evidence alone.

From 1847 to the present, scientists have recorded increasing numbers of shallow, crater-like depressions scattered around Carolina and into northern Florida. There are now known to be some 500,000 of them, of which approximately 140,000 have long-axis diameters greater than 500 feet. They are known as the Carolina Bays.

Those bays which have been investigated in North Carolina show traces of meteoric iron. This, and finds of actual meteorites in and around the bays, has led scientists, among them F. A. Melton, W. Schriever and Henry Savage Jr, to conclude they were the result of a massive meteor bombardment . . . at the end of the Pleistocene era.

Similar shallow depressions, presumably of like origin, exist in Alaska, Siberia, Bolivia and the Netherlands.

On South Island, New Zealand, a Maori tradition recalls how, long ago, a glowing object appeared in the sky, then shattered, showering the Earth with devastating fragments. There are indications that the tradition is more than a myth. Huge quantities of 'China stones' – which contain the burned remains of late Pleistocene plants – and metallic objects, apparently of meteoric origin, have been found scattered across a broad sweep of the island.

In their scholarly work *When the Earth Nearly Died*,[39] authors D. S. Allan and J. B. Delair make the interesting suggestion that the Book of Revelation is not a wholly predictive work or mystical vision, but contains elements of a tradition engendered by the catastrophe of Vela-F. If so, this unlikely source brings some interesting detail to the picture.

Revelation 18:11–19, for example, appears to be a description of the world as it was before disaster struck – and immediately after. The text reads:

> And the merchants of the earth shall weep and mourn
> . . . for no man buyeth their merchandise any more:
> The merchandise of gold, and silver, and precious
> stones, and of pearls, and fine linen, and purple, and
> silk, and scarlet, and all thyine wood, and all manner
> vessels of ivory, and all manner vessels of most precious

---

[39] Gateway Books, Bath, England, 1995.

wood, and of brass, and iron, and marble: And cinnamon, and odours, and ointments, and frankincense, and wine, and oil, and fine flour, and wheat, and beasts, and sheep, and horses, and chariots, and slaves, and souls of men. And the fruits that thy soul lusted after are departed from thee, and all things which were dainty and godly are departed from thee, and thou shalt find them no more at all. The merchants of these things, which were made rich . . . shall stand afar off . . . weeping and wailing, and saying, Alas, alas that great city, that was clothed in fine linen, and purple, and scarlet, and decked with gold, and precious stones, and pearls! For in one hour so great riches is come to nought. And every shipmaster, and all the company in ships, and sailors, and as many as trade by sea, stood afar off, and cried when they saw the smoke . . . saying, What city is like unto this great city! And they cast dust on their heads, and cried, weeping and wailing, saying, Alas, alas that great city, wherein were made rich all that had ships in the sea by reason of her costliness! for in one hour is she made desolate.

Quite clearly, this refers to a substantial maritime civilisation with an economy based on extensive trading, identical to that postulated by Hapgood in his investigation of the maps of his ancient sea kings. But it was a civilisation that ended abruptly – 'in one hour' – and seems to have ended in flames. What started the fires may be hinted at in Revelation 11:13:

And the same hour there was a great earthquake, and the tenth part of the city fell, and in the earthquake were slain of men seven thousand: and the remnant were affrighted . . .

But the earthquake was seen as just one of a series of 'woes' visited by God on humanity. These included 'lightnings, and voices, and thunderings, and an earthquake, and great hail' – almost an exact description of the events we have just been examining.

Interestingly, the biblical account links these phenomena with the appearance of 'a great wonder in heaven'. The description is heavily symbolic, but beneath the symbolism we may discern actual astronomical events. Revelation 12:1–4 reads:

> And there appeared a great wonder in heaven; a woman clothed with the sun, and the moon under her feet, and upon her head a crown of twelve stars . . . And there appeared another wonder in heaven; and behold a great red dragon, having seven heads and ten horns, and seven crowns upon his heads. And his tail drew the third part of the stars of heaven, and did cast them to the earth . . .

The term 'clothed with the sun' suggests a fiery, shining body which appeared in the night sky dwarfing the moon ('the moon under her feet'). The crown of twelve stars may refer to the fragments of the exploded planet that accompanied Vela-F, which would have the appearance of stars in the same way that meteorites have earned the description 'shooting stars'. The great red dragon could be a particularly large fragment, a captured moon from one of the outer planets or even the original Vela-F body itself. Taking the verses together, it is clear that what is being described is two large celestial bodies which appeared, more or less simultaneously, in the skies above Earth, accompanied by several smaller companions.

Here again, the similarity with the Vela-F reconstruction is striking, especially when we read that the 'tail of the dragon' drew stars from heaven and cast them to the Earth – a description of the great meteor bombardment.

Here, as elsewhere, it is important to remember the mindset of our distant ancestors when faced with astronomical phenomena. All early cultures saw the planets and the stars as gods, but a Christianised account of an ancient legend would almost routinely substitute 'God' and his 'angels' for the original pantheistic concept. Thus it is no surprise to find the battle of Chakekenapok and Manibozho, the great conflict of the planetary gods, the Babylonian fight between Marduk and Tiamat, described in familiar religious terms, quoted here from Revelation 12:7–12:

> And there was war in heaven: Michael and his angels fought against the dragon; and the dragon fought and his angels, and prevailed not; neither was their place found any more in heaven. And the great dragon was cast out, that old serpent, called the Devil, and Satan, which deceiveth the whole world: he was cast out into the earth, and his angels were cast out with him. Therefore rejoice, ye heavens, and ye that dwell in them. Woe to the inhabitors of the earth and of the sea! for the devil is come down unto you, having great wrath, because he knoweth that he hath but a short time.

Once you look beyond the symbolism, the astronomical elements are all there. Two cosmic bodies come into close proximity and conflict, like the Vela-F intruder and the giant planet beyond the orbit of Mars. The suggestion that 'their place was found not any more in heaven' speaks volumes of two facts. The first is that a familiar planet ceased to be seen in the night sky. The second is that the intruder itself disappeared as well, either by leaving our solar system or by crashing into the sun.

But those who watched terrified as the disaster unfolded would not necessarily have interpreted it in the terms we would use today. As giant meteors rained down, they could have concluded that Vela-F was being hurled to Earth, and indeed, we have little idea of how massive any given meteor may have been at that time.

From the viewpoint of the observers, the result had to be cause for rejoicing in the heavens since the sky was well rid of the intruding troublemaker. But the same could not be said for Earth, because it seemed as if the intruder – the personification of all evil – had been imprisoned beneath the tortured surface of our planet . . . and might well emerge again at some point in the future.

Elsewhere in Revelation, a sequence of cataclysmic events is outlined – again well wrapped in religious symbolism – that is disturbingly close to the picture we have already been examining. Speaking of angels, Revelation 16:2–21 states:

> And the first [angel] went, and poured out his vial upon the earth; and there fell a noisome and grievous sore upon the men . . . And the second angel poured out his vial upon the sea; and it became as the blood of a dead man: and every living soul died in the sea . . . And the third angel poured out his vial upon the rivers and fountains of waters; and they became blood . . . And the fourth angel poured out his vial upon the sun; and power was given unto him to scorch men with fire. And men were scorched with great heat, and blasphemed the name of God, which hath power over these plagues: and they repented not to give him glory. And the fifth angel poured out his vial upon the seat of the beast; and his kingdom was full of darkness; and they gnawed their tongues for pain, and blasphemed the God of heaven because of their pains and their sores, and repented not of their deeds. And the sixth angel poured out his vial upon the great river Euphrates; and

the water thereof was dried up . . . And the seventh
angel poured out his vial into the air; and there came
a great voice out of the temple of heaven, from the
throne, saying, It is done. And there were voices, and
thunders, and lightnings; and there was a great earthquake, such as was not since men were upon the earth,
so mighty an earthquake, and so great. And the great
city was divided into three parts, and the cities of the
nations fell . . . And every island fled away, and the
mountains were not found. And there fell upon men a
great hail out of heaven, every stone about the weight
of a talent: and men blasphemed God because of the
plague of the hail; for the plague thereof was exceed-
ing great.

Continuing with extracts from Revelation 17:21 and 21:1, we
learn:

And a mighty angel took up a stone like a great millstone, and cast it into the sea . . . And I saw a new
heaven and a new earth: for the first heaven and the
first earth were passed away; and there was no more
sea.

Familiar elements come thick and fast in this quoted passage. The
catastrophe, which involved constant earthquakes, volcanic
eruptions, planetary typhoons and cosmic lightning bolts was
nothing if not 'noisome'. The sea, rivers and fountains of 'blood'
is reminiscent of the enormous red-hot lava flows that followed
the massive fracturing of the Earth, although the writer might
equally well mean the pollution of the waterways that would
have inevitably followed the tectonic disturbances.

Scorching heat, here attributed to the sun, was certainly an element of the disaster, as was the Stygian darkness that followed

atmospheric pollution from volcanic ash. Incredibly, the description also manages to pinpoint yet another aspect of the disaster, as tectonic plate shifts and subductions began to alter ancient water courses. The great Euphrates, and many other rivers, may well have temporarily run dry.

The disruption of our atmosphere arose from the sudden speeding up of the planet's period of rotation rather than the contents of an angel's vial, but there was certainly thunder and lightning, and the howling of a wind that must have sounded like a million voices.

The unusually violent earthquake, part of a series that wracked the entire globe, is also mentioned, as is the destruction of the world's cities, now buried so deeply by the disaster that they are lost to archaeology. As the Earth's crust buckled and heaved, islands – possibly including Plato's island kingdom of Atlantis – did indeed disappear, as did the ancient mountain chains replaced by new, higher, violently upthrust ranges.

The meteorite bombardment may have been what is here referred to as 'hail', although as we shall see, there may have been a more literal source for the description. The fall of a massive meteorite is certainly embodied in the legend of an angel hurling a millstone. No wonder the writer speaks of a new heaven and new Earth. The old planetary order of our solar system had been swept away by the Vela intruder and the surface of our planet changed for ever. Even the familiar seas had drained to different basins. But possibly not for long. In Revelation 12 and 14, the account goes on:

And the serpent cast out of his mouth water as a flood . . . and the earth opened her mouth, and swallowed up the flood which the dragon cast out of his mouth . . . And I heard a voice from heaven, as the voice of many waters . . .

The apocryphal Book of Enoch insists these events occurred at a time when 'the Ark floated on the waters'. Is it possible the cataclysm engendered by Vela-F was somehow connected with the biblical Flood?

20

DELUGE AND FLOOD

—————————— FACT ——————————

WHEN THE STANDING WAVE BROKE, THE FLOW
BECAME A RAGING TORRENT FAR BEYOND ANYTHING IN
HUMAN EXPERIENCE BEFORE OR SINCE. THE WALL OF
WATER WAS WHAT LIFTED THE ERRATICS.

The tilting of the Earth's axis by the massive gravitational field of Vela-F strongly suggests that the intruder made its closest pass to our planet over one or other of the polar regions. Other evidence narrows possibilities to the northlands.

As Vela-F moved ever closer, ocean waters, already disrupted by the massive tectonic activity, now began to flow northwards in response to the inexorable gravitational pull of the intruder. This was tidal action, but on an unprecedented scale.

Today, the moon influences all the world's seas and oceans, drawing them over huge expanses of land with each high tide. Vela-F was not just larger than our moon, but more than 100 times larger than the Earth. Not only that, but its flight path actually brought it much closer to the Earth than the moon is now. The gravitational forces were enormous.

Some 70.8 per cent of the Earth's surface is covered by water to an average depth of 12,447 feet. The mass of the oceans is approximately $\frac{1}{4400}$ (one four-thousand-four-hundredth) of the total mass of the Earth. This vast quantity of water forms what oceanographers refer to as the World Ocean. (Our convenient sub-division into the various oceans and seas is largely arbitrary.) It was on the World Ocean as a whole that Vela-F exerted its baleful tidal pull, drawing unimaginable quantities of water further and further northwards.

As gravitational action peaked, a phenomenon occurred that is not only unknown today, but is literally impossible today. The waters of the world began to pile up in a gigantic standing wave, sucked towards the immense fiery mass that now filled the heavens.

The northlands themselves were growing cold. Earth's axial tilt had carried them abruptly out of the old temperate zone and faced them away from the warmth of the sun. With the world's volcanoes spewing ash and other pollutants into the atmosphere, there was a further blocking of sunlight and heat. Yet the intruder itself was adding its radiation to that of the sun and tectonic activity was adding more heat locally across the globe. The result of this unusual set of circumstances – in particular the collection of water droplets around atmospheric particles – was rain, a driving deluge whipped by the constant hurricane-force winds. This rain, which fell as snow in northern regions, was the reality behind the familiar biblical account:

> And God said unto Noah, The end of all flesh is come before me; for the earth is filled with violence through them; and, behold, I will destroy them with the earth . . . For yet seven days, and I will cause it to rain upon the earth forty days and forty nights; and every living substance that I have made will I destroy from off the face of the earth.

It is interesting to note the echo of Plato in this passage from

Genesis 6:13 and 7:4. The Greek philosopher claimed that the warlike ambitions of the Atlantean kings displeased their gods and the destruction of their continent followed shortly. Archaeological and geological evidence both suggest the Vela-F disaster followed the first major war in human history. Now, in Genesis 7:10–12 the same theme appears since it is human violence that occasions God's displeasure.

> And it came to pass after seven days, that . . . were all the fountains of the great deep broken up, and the windows of heaven were opened. And the rain was upon the earth forty days and forty nights.

This account of the Deluge (Genesis 7: 17–19) gives the clear impression that it was the heavy rain that caused the universal Flood:

> And the flood was forty days upon the earth; and the waters increased, and bare up the ark, and it was lift up above the earth. And the waters prevailed, and were increased greatly upon the earth; and the ark went upon the face of the waters. And the waters prevailed exceedingly upon the earth . . .

In the passage above there is more than a hint of gradual flooding, with the ark slowly lifted by the rising waters. Given the violence and extent of the storm in a world unused to precipitation, it is no surprise that the writer of Genesis concluded there was a causal connection between the Deluge and the Flood.

But while the Deluge certainly preceded the Flood, it did not cause it. What happened was infinitely more dramatic – and destructive – than any slowly rising waters.

As Vela-F, and any remaining companions, continued on its trajectory towards Venus, the immense gravitational field lessened with distance. In the northlands of a rain-swept world, the locked seawaters of the planet began to free themselves. The standing wave broke. As the celestial intruder disappeared, the real Flood began.

The Flood story, as it appears in the Koran, is closer to this reality, telling how the Ark swam between waves 'like mountains'. When Noah's son decided to seek refuge outside the Ark, Noah warned him there was no security to be had anywhere, except for those on whom God would show mercy, and watched helpless as he was carried away by another wave. This is not a description of gently rising waters.

Choctaw and Navajo legends tell a truly chilling tale of this time. After a long period of darkness, a light appeared in the north. At first it must have seemed like a salvation, but then a stampede of wild animals appeared, fleeing in panic. Scouts were sent to investigate and returned with terrifying news. A mountain of water was bearing down on them. Soon the flood filled the entire horizon on three sides, a veritable wall of water sweeping the land like the wrath of God.

The immense flow of water back from the northlands must have begun slowly at first, but increased as the gravitational field weakened. When the standing wave broke, the flow became a raging torrent far beyond anything in human experience before or since.

The wall of water was what lifted the erratics. In 1877, a gale in northern Scotland whipped up waves sufficiently strong to carry away a pier weighing 2,600 tons, so there is little doubt about the ability of this incomparably greater mass of water to move vast loads great distances across the land.

This gigantic flood did not have the physical problems of glaciers in climbing hills and even mountains – it simply broke over them like a giant wave, depositing debris on their northern aspect and often mimicking the scour of ice on rock strata. The memory of the event is there in Genesis 7: 19–24.

> . . . and all the high hills, that were under the whole
> heaven, were covered . . . and the mountains were
> covered. And all flesh died that moved upon the earth,
> both of fowl, and of cattle, and of beast, and of every
> creeping thing that creepeth upon the earth, and every
> man: And the waters prevailed upon the earth an
> hundred and fifty days.

Since mountain crests can today be measured literally in miles, the idea of a flood sufficiently deep to cover them has long been met with incredulity by secular scientists. But what is important here is not the final depth of the waters, but rather their wave action as they bore down from the north. Giant walls of water crashing down could well swamp entire mountains, at least temporarily. An early legend in the Jewish Haggadah may actually recall the original standing wave held by the gravitational field of the Vela intruder. It describes 'waters piled up to a height of 1,600 miles' that could be seen by 'all nations of the Earth'.

Quite clearly the destructive power of such a mass of water would vary in relation to local geography and factors like distance from the source. Were this not so, it is difficult to see how any life on Earth could have survived. As it was, civilisation was utterly destroyed and a remnant humanity took refuge not only in arks – a near universal tradition – but in caves and caverns on high ground. It is probable that survivors actually took refuge not from the flood, but from the storms, heat and meteoric bombardment that preceded it.

Navajo Indian folklore describes a time when 'all the nations'[40] lived underground in the heart of a mountain. They had plenty of game since their refuge was shared by great numbers of wild animals. This happened at a time of near darkness when the sun

---

[40] The term is apparently meant to go beyond the Native American nations of Plain Indians since it includes white people.

emerged dimly for no more than a few hours each day. Their
entrance may have been sealed by the wave-borne debris. The legend tells how the people had to dig themselves out. When they
did so, they found their mountain surrounded by a lake of water
as far as the eye could see.

The Navajo tale incorporates another element frequently found
in the lore of other races, including the biblical account of the
Tower of Babel. While all those in the cavern spoke a single language, they began to speak different tongues when they emerged.
The world that greeted them was still dim and persistent cloud
cover – or pollution haze – blotted out the moon and stars. But
at least the floodwater receded fairly quickly.

Left to its own devices, water flows to the lowest available level.
While the planetary tidal wave that followed the departure of
Vela-F was probably the most destructive phenomenon ever
experienced on the face of the Earth, it would by its very nature
be fairly short-lived. Here again, Genesis 8: 1–14 is in accord
with a rational analysis of the situation:

> And God made a wind to pass over the earth, and the
> waters assuaged; The fountains also of the deep and
> the windows of heaven were stopped, and the rain
> from heaven was restrained; And the waters returned
> from off the earth continually; and after the end of the
> hundred and fifty days the waters were abated . . . And
> the waters decreased continually until the tenth month:
> in the tenth month, on the first day of the month, were
> the tops of the mountains seen. And it came to pass at
> the end of forty days, that Noah opened the window
> of the ark which he had made: And he sent forth a
> raven, which went forth to and fro, until the waters
> were dried up from off the earth . . . And it came to
> pass in the six hundredth and first year, in the first
> month, the first day of the month, the waters were dried

up from off the earth: and Noah removed the covering of the ark, and looked, and, behold, the face of the
ground was dry. And in the second month, on the seven
and twentieth day of the month, was the earth dried.

As the floodwaters drained to form new seas and oceans in the
freshly created basins of a tortured Earth, humanity emerged from
its worst nightmare into a broken, desolate world. The myths of
peoples from Scandinavia to the Near East to North America
carry folk memories of the scene. Mud was everywhere. The lush,
abundant vegetation of the Golden Age was obliterated. Much of
the underlying land had been sterilised by lava. Whole forests had
been flattened by the planetary hurricane. Even the mud was infer-
tile. As the waters dried, survivors noted the white coating of salt.
    Ironically, the most immediate problem was thirst. Those
springs that had not been turned brackish by the flood were polluted by volcanic fumes. According to a British Colombian tradition, people came close to dying for lack of drinking water.
Fortunately the world's weather was still far from settled.
Although the worst of the wind had died down and the heavier
elements of pollution were gradually clearing from the air, the climate was still a million miles away from its old stability. More
torrential rain began to fall. Fresh water once again collected.
    But by this stage in the disaster, it is no longer possible to talk
in global terms. Local variation of terrain, watercourses, remnant
tectonic activity, and weather made the difference to whether
people lived or died. For a time at least there was protein to be
scavenged from the bodies of billions of dead animals strewn
across the globe, but in the warmer regions these would have
begun to rot within days. Elsewhere, one might speculate that the
salt layer which poisoned the land and polluted the drinking water
may actually have acted to preserve some of the meat.
    This factor – and the probability that a few areas of the globe
may have been spared the worst tribulations of the disaster – could

well have proven the salvation of our race. By the time the salted food stocks began to perish, plant growth may have begun to re-establish. A Babylonian legend claims humanity ate only couch-grass for a year – a literal impossibility, but a tradition that under-lines the tenacious nature of some grasses that can reappear on, for example, newly formed lava beds in a matter of months.

All the same, humanity must have been decimated and brutally demoralised by the disaster. It is as well to remind ourselves that prior to the appearance of Vela-F, vast numbers of our ancestors had for generations been accustomed to the comforts of civilisa-tion and were thus ill-equipped for this sudden plunge into a stark survival situation. It is safe to say that of the few millions world-wide who survived the immediate disaster, many hundreds of thousands must have died from hunger, thirst and in all proba-bility disease, in the immediate aftermath. And those fortunates who made it past the first intensely dangerous weeks and months soon found themselves facing yet another peril. The Ice Age, that great myth of the Pleistocene, arrived at last.

21

AFTERMATH
OF DISASTER

FACT

IN SHORT, FLINT BECAME THE TECHNICAL

FOUNDATION OF A WHOLE NEW CULTURE. THE

STONE AGE HAD BEGUN.

Among the most convincing evidence that Revelation does indeed incorporate elements of an ancient catastrophic tradition is one of its most obscure passages:

> And I saw as it were a sea of glass mingled with fire: and them that had gotten the victory . . . stand on the sea of glass . . .[41]

The highly visual description of a 'sea of glass' calls to mind Agassiz's term *mer de glace* – his (largely imaginary) sea of ice. As earthquakes and volcanic eruptions continued – albeit at a decreased level – in the aftermath of the great disaster, did human

---

[41] Rev. 15:2.

eyes record that curious mixture of fire and ice as lava oozed up through a glacial field?

The Deluge that drenched the southern latitudes fell as snow in the northlands. Earth's axial shift carried the ancient temperate zone with its sweeping forests, fertile plains and teeming game, into the chill darkness of an Arctic night. The transition was abrupt. In Siberia, mammoths were flash-frozen where they stood, the grasses of their last meal half digested in their stomachs.

As the world's seas and oceans were drawn inexorably northwards, the sheer volume of water and the latent heat it stored guaranteed immunity from freezing. But once Vela-F passed on, the standing wave broke and the World Ocean again drained southwards, the northernmost remnants of the great primeval Flood quickly froze to solid ice.

This brand new polar ice cap was just one factor in a rapidly changing global climate. The massive heat-generating volcanic activity gradually subsided, but particle ash content of the atmosphere remained high. (In modern times, the explosive eruption of Krakatoa produced atmospheric ash that remained in suspension, producing glorious sunsets, for more than three years.) The days of total darkness may have ended, but sunlight throughout the world was dimmed – and would remain so for many years.

As the heat radiation from the intruder itself diminished with distance, temperatures began to drop in every continent.

Chapter 8 outlined the unusual conditions needed for an Ice Age. The first prerequisite is heat, which evaporates the water necessary to make ice. Next you need precipitation – so long as moisture remains locked in the atmosphere, no ice forms. Finally, you need a period of prolonged, widespread and intense cold. The Vela disaster provided every ingredient.

In the initial high-tectonic stage when floodplains of lava flowed and heat radiation from Vela-F was added to that of the sun, traditions throughout the world refer to rivers and lakes so overheated that they actually boiled. This heat evaporated the · water needed for rain. Pollution particles provided the nucleus around which droplets formed. Cyclonic winds carried the rains across the globe. Then the temperature dropped and stayed low for years.

Another factor in the development of this belated Ice Age was the appearance of high mountain ranges. Unlike the Polar mountains evoked by nineteenth-century scientists, the world's mountains were solid, massive, real and, above all, high. They acted as glacier generators exactly as Agassiz and the others speculated.

Freed of the necessity to explain the effects of deluge and flood, it now becomes possible to envisage glacial movement that no longer contradicts the laws of physics. Huge continental ice sheets of the type envisaged by Agassiz remain unlikely (and unnecessary) but extensive glacier flow is not. The memory of it appears in the Norse mythology of a dreadful Fimbul Winter, in the Polynesian tradition of a curdled, icy ocean, in the Peruvian legend that the gods spread snow and ice across the land once the great universal Flood receded.

Some species lived, some died. Since there is no evidence of any particular geographical distribution in those which perished, we need to look for the reasons elsewhere. One factor may have been size.

In the immediate aftermath of the cataclysm, vegetation was scarce. Although plant growth recovered eventually, it did not recover quickly enough for the big browsers. Mammoth and mastodon are animals that require literally tons of vegetation to sustain themselves. There was simply no substitute. They and the other vegetarian heavyweights, like the auroch ox and the giant sloth, died in their millions.

Fussy eaters went too. In Australia today, the koala bear lives on an exclusive diet of eucalyptus leaves. If the eucalyptus trees in its range die out for any reason, the koalas die too, however many other species of trees, plants, nuts or fruit remain around them. Their metabolism has specifically adapted to one food source, and one only. Niche-feeders of this type which existed in the Pleistocene are likely to have died even faster than the big browsers, whatever their size.

Hunters unwilling to eat carrion died with their prey species. The tally here included the ferocious sabre-toothed cats and the massive dire-wolf. Best fitted to survive were the insects (that need so little in the way of food), the sea creatures (whose habitat was disrupted, but not ruined), the scavengers, the ruthless, the adaptable, the cunning and the just plain lucky. Against this sorry background, humanity struggled on.

There were very few of us about. The teeming millions of the old world population had been decimated by earthquake, by lava flow, by landslide, aerial bombardment, deluge, flood and finally starvation. As the Navajo recorded, the survivors crawled from their shelters to survey a drowned world.

When the floodwaters receded, the new environment was both unfamiliar and brutally hostile. In colder climes, the natural deep-freeze provided a larder of fast-frozen carcasses to eat, but in the temperate regions this multitude of corpses – animal and human – strewn across the barren, muddy landscape soon began to putrefy with an accompanying all-pervasive stench and an ever-increasing risk of disease. Only the devastating drop in population prevented the sort of widespread plagues that characterised the Middle Ages. Humanity now huddled in small, isolated communities. Plagues did not, could not, spread.

The most immediate necessity, echoed in God's words to Jacob, was to be fruitful and multiply. Humanity's salvation depended utterly on repopulating an empty world. But multiplication was only possible in a supportive environment. New mouths to feed required the food to feed them. In a world almost stripped of its plant cover and its abundant herds of game, a nomadic lifestyle became the only viable option. Necessity turned us into wandering hunter-gatherers.

Many of these isolated colonies migrated to the newly contoured seashores. There must have been a superstitious dread of water, but it was balanced by the fact that across the face of our shattered, chilling planet, only the oceans still teemed with life. Shell middens along the coastlines of every continent testify to how much our ancestors relied on seafood for support.

There was much to learn. The cave paintings of antediluvian peoples indicate they wore few, if any, clothes. This custom, now so often viewed as 'primitive', was no more than a response to a benign, intensely humid climate. But now the climate had changed. Warm clothing was a sudden necessity. For many, this meant learning the skill of the tailor.

But the skill of the tailor was just one of the many skills required to meet the challenge of a new and hostile world. Imagine how matters would be if our own civilisation was destroyed in a matter of days or weeks. Those of us who once threw a switch to produce light, create warmth or cook food, would have to learn the trick of making fire – without disposable lighters or a box of matches. For most of us, our most prized skills and experience would suddenly be useless. The only things that would matter would be physical strength, good health, endurance and the bedrock abilities that ensure survival in a nomadic, hunter-gatherer community.

With their familiar tools and weapons swept away, our immediate post-diluvian ancestors turned, perhaps in desperation, to whatever was at hand. Among the most common and useful materials was flint. Flint could be split and chipped to produce blades sharper than any honed metal – and if the edge was soon lost, a new blade could easily be fashioned.

Flint had a multitude of uses. In spearheads and arrowheads it could be used to hunt the rapidly expanding herds of game. (Once vegetation recovered, rapid expansion of fauna was inevitable in open, empty ranges low on both predators and competition.) It could be used to butcher kills, skin animals for their pelts. It could be used in weaponry for offence and defence. In short, flint became the technical foundation of a whole new culture. The Stone Age had begun.

Throughout the world, there were survivors who inherited certain relevant skills and knowledge from pre-Flood times. Their existence is recorded in the folklore and mythology of every continent. They were the teachers whose contribution was so great and wisdom so important that they were deified by their companions.

In 1967, a Swiss author, Erich Von Däniken, studied these and other myths, noted the all-too-mundane characteristics of these 'gods' and decided they must have come from outer space. Their actual home was more down-to-earth, although the culture that produced them had suddenly become as inaccessible as another planet.

These teachers worked hard, and sometimes travelled far, in their attempt to re-establish civilisation. They were law-givers who laid down precepts for good government and fair judgement. They taught useful arts and crafts. In many areas their input must

have made the difference between the survival or disappearance
of a precious community.

Not all their knowledge could be put to use. Shipbuilding skills
may have been preserved, but what use would they be in a world
without wood? The ancient timber forests must have taken many
human generations to regenerate. In an environment where the
only real priority was sheer survival, mining, smelting and metalworking, architecture, monumental engineering and a thousand
other skills were simply no longer relevant.

The teachers concentrated on only one thing beyond immediate survival needs – the revival of farming. Over and over again,
world mythologies stress how tutelary deities taught primitive
humanity sowing, reaping and the domestication of certain
animals like cattle, sheep, horses, pigs and, later, fowl. And it is
a fact of orthodox archaeology that the agricultural revolution was
humanity's first and earliest step upwards.

It is also a fact, far less noted by modern scholars, that the
development of agriculture – which seems to have occurred spon-
taneously in different areas – exhibits a curious pattern. In many
locations, it seems to have begun on high ground and spread
outwards – not at all what one might expect if the only criteria
was suitable ground.

Although their influence was necessarily limited in the immediate aftermath of the Flood, and for many generations thereafter,
it seems almost certain that the teachers preserved a tradition
of ancient skills against the time when they might once again be
of use to humanity.

The idea of an initiate elite carefully recording, memorising
and passing on such an ancient body of knowledge is a
romantic one. But it remains the best explanation of the sudden
flowering of developed architectural and engineering skills in,
for example, Old Kingdom Egypt.

In this context it is interesting to note that Egypt's arts of architecture and engineering were held to stem from Imhotep, a fabled

advisor to the Third Dynasty's King Zoser. Imhotep was so respected for his skills that he was accorded the stature of a god, exactly like the great post-diluvian teachers who preceded him. He was also supposed to have been the son of Ptah; one of Egypt's most important deities who was regarded as the patron of metal-workers, artisans and medicine.

The Ice Age that once seized our world was far more short-lived than modern science credits. It began to lose its grip perhaps as early as 8000 BC and the last of its ravages disappeared in a period of general global warming some 2,000 years later.

Freed of the problems engendered by the ice, the direct intel-lectual (and possibly genetic) descendants of those survivors who held themselves as guardians of the ancient science and technol-ogy began to release more and more of their wisdom. These were no abstract philosophies, but practical techniques that helped con-struct the pyramids and place trading ships once again on the oceans of the world.

The great maritime civilisation postulated by Hapgood and Plato had disappeared, perhaps, as Plato claimed, into the new depths of a post-diluvian Atlantic. Ur-Athens was no more, swal-lowed up by the mighty tectonic convulsions that marked the first close approach of Vela-F. Even the proto-civilisation of ancient Egypt was buried too deeply for the reach of modern archaeolo-gists, except for a few isolated items like the statue of the sphinx at Giza.

Yet something of the old ways obviously survived. A traumat-ised humanity began the long haul upwards.

EPILOGUE

Plato described Atlantis as a civilisation not really all that different from ancient Egypt, Greece or Rome. Others aren't so sure.

An American politician recently expressed the opinion that the real cause of Atlantis sinking was a laser war between two of its opposing factions. The military technology got out of hand and the continent broke apart. Another American, the famous 'sleeping prophet', Edgar Cayce, built up a comprehensive picture of the lost continent over literally thousands of 'life-readings' – psychical investigations of patients' early (re)incarnations. These indicated a crystal-based technology far in advance of anything seen on Earth up to and including the present day.

The occultist Helena Petrovna Blavatsky, who founded the Theosophical movement, taught that the Atlanteans had evolved a form of genetic engineering which enabled them to breed a sub-human slave race.

Arthur Desmond Leslie suspects the Atlanteans were sufficiently advanced to develop *vimanas* – mercury-powered aircraft described in ancient Hindu religious texts.

Our own civilisation has, of course, managed to develop aircraft, lasers and genetic engineering. It is also crystal based to a degree few people realise. Without crystals your watch would stop, your computer grind to a halt, your radio and television shut off and your house fall down. Almost all of today's more commonplace devices have a crystal of one sort or another as a vital component, and the cement so fundamental to modern engineering sets as the result of crystalline action.

Despite this, even scholars sympathetic to the idea of a lost civilisation draw the line at accepting a lost *hi-tech* civilisation. The concept is almost too ludicrous to warrant serious investigation.

Our earliest datable source of information on how the ancient Hebrews organised time is an inscription known as the Gezer Calendar. It was written in the late tenth century BC, the reign of Solomon, and describes the time allocated to the major agricultural tasks within a cycle of twelve moons. The Hebrew term *yereah* denotes both 'moon' and 'month'. A second Hebrew term for month, *hodesh*, is literally translated as the 'newness of the lunar crescent'. On this basis it is clear that the earliest Hebrew calendar was lunar based, as it remains, essentially, to this day.

One reason why so few ancient nations followed the Hebrew example is the extraordinary difficulties experienced in calculating – or indeed even measuring – the precise length of the lunar cycle. The problem is that each lunar orbit of the Earth is unique. It always differs slightly from the last.

In the broader picture, the moon returns to its exact original starting point as measured against the sun only once in 687,282 years. This makes even the calculation of an average lunar orbit something of a nightmare. The near approximation in general use by astronomers today requires the solution of an equation of more than 6,000 terms – thankfully tackled only by computers.

Despite the problems, the ancient Hebrews made their own stab at it. The result forms part of an oral rabbinical tradition that survived long enough to be eventually recorded in writing and is thus available for examination today. The figure they arrived at described an average lunar cycle as consisting of 29.53059 days. Until 1968, this was the exact figure reached by twentieth-century scientists using the best available observational data and computer power. Even today, corrections have led to a new value that differs from the ancient Hebrew calculation by no more than two parts in a million.

There is absolute evidence that the Hebrew figure for the lunar orbit was in place in the first century BC, and general scholarly acceptance that it was known long before. The mystery is how, with no astronomical tradition worth mentioning, the Hebrews managed to reach it.

The usual answer is that they picked it up from the Babylonians, who did have a profound knowledge of astronomy. Unfortunately for this theory, the Babylonian figure is also known and differs from the Hebrew . . . as does the Greek – another possibility often mooted. In each case, the Hebrew figure, while close, is more accurate.

But if not from the Babylonians or Greeks, then where? The oral tradition is in no doubt whatsoever. The wherewithal to calculate this astonishingly accurate value was given by God Himself to the prophet Moses and enshrined in the Torah, the first five divinely transmitted books of the Old Testament.

This charming fiction was roundly ignored by scientists – whose preference has always been to keep God out of their calculations – and even by scholars who could find no indication in the Torah, or anywhere else for that matter, of a method that would give rise to this result. Apart from the devout, the only people to take the tradition remotely seriously were the Qabalists, a mystic-minded group, often themselves rabbis, who spent their lives searching for secrets hidden in the Scriptures. One of them, Rabbi Moses ben Maimon, actually claimed the method was *coded* within the Torah.

Rabbi ben Maimon – better known as Maimonides – came to be revered as Judaism's greatest sage, but even his towering prestige was not enough to persuade the scientific community that the idea of a Torah code should be taken seriously. At least, not until the 1980s when computer analysis showed such a code actually existed.

The 'Bible Code', as it is now generally known, is the name applied to sequences of cipher hidden within the original Hebrew Torah. These sequences not only included the moon orbit calculation Maimonides claimed – based on the fact that each letter of the Hebrew alphabet has an attributed numerical value – but also referred to such Jewish holidays as Hanukkah and Purim. It was these latter coded references that lit the fuse on a time bomb.

The Torah will be more generally familiar to non-Jewish readers as the first five books of the Old Testament – Genesis, Exodus, Leviticus, Numbers and Deuteronomy – the authorship of which is traditionally attributed to Moses. A Hebrew oral tradition is more explicit. These Books, it is held, were not written by Moses, but by God. Moses was only involved in taking them down as dictation.

Although there is some controversy about the actual dating, the time of Moses is now generally attributed to the thirteenth century BC, but a great many scholars have questioned whether he had very much to do with the Torah, either as its author or as God's secretary. They point to difficulties like the fact that Moses was apparently able to record his own death and evidence that the Books are not the work of a single author, but a pastiche of several different literary sources.

Even so, proponents of this viewpoint are more or less united in their conviction that the scriptures date no later than the end of the Babylonian exile, around 500 BC. But while the later date of 500 BC might just possibly account for the mention of Purim, which celebrates the survival of Jews marked for death by their Persian rulers in the fifth century BC, it remains a mystery how this ancient text could encode the holiday of Hanukkah which celebrates a Jewish uprising in 164 BC – more than 300 years later.

Scientists working on the material swiftly determined that this encoding was no freak. The names of more than sixty Jewish sages, cross-referenced with their birth or death dates and their cities of residence, have been found encoded in the Torah, although they all lived many centuries after it was written. Incredible though it might seem, the code has a predictive element.

As news of the scientific work began to spread, it was inevitable that the discovery would be sensationalised. Several attempts have been made to use the code as an oracle to prophesy our own future. Unfortunately – or perhaps fortunately – the structure of the code does not lend itself to this sort of amateur fortune-telling. In essence, you have to know what you are looking for before current decoding methods (which are heavily statistically based) can be applied. Thus the code can confirm past events – albeit those that took place *after* the Torah was written – but cannot predict events yet to come.

Disappointing though this may be, the fact that a predictive element is there at all has had a profound influence on the minds of those scientists working seriously on Bible Code analysis. Although the majority are Jewish by race, a great many began their study as religious agnostics or athesists. But once they discovered that the code was genuine and, particularly, that it contained predictive elements, there has been a low-key but distinct tendency to return to strict religious observance. In short, even the scientists are beginning to suspect what the rabbis have long claimed: that the Torah was literally written by God.

This type of polarisation is understandable, even predictable. The religious tradition carries the weight of centuries and (often) the force of childhood conditioning. But attractive though this makes it, there are problems.

Among them is the fact that while the lunar orbit calculation leads to a figure of astonishing accuracy, it is still less accurate than the figure in use today. What improved the old calculation was satellite technology. Observations made from orbiting satellites have helped us improve on what purports to be knowledge handed down directly from God.

Yet the code remains a reality and its predictive element remains a reality. Both are extremely difficult to explain – so difficult in fact that one can sympathise with the assumption that they must represent the work of a divine hand. All the same, Occam's Razor denies us the right to invoke a complex explanation when a simple one will suffice, an unlikely explanation where a more likely one will do. If you hear hoof beats behind you in Britain, Europe or America, the most likely explanation is an approaching horse. Only in Africa are you likely to turn to face a zebra.

In the case of the Torah Code, the divine explanation is substantially more exotic than the theory that this encoding, bizarre though it might be, is the work of human hands. But it is only now that we might speculate on whose.

The orthodox picture of prehistory, to which many scientists investigating the code subscribe, insists that ancient Israel was, by comparison with its modern counterpart, a primitive place in a primitive world that had evolved from an even more primitive past.

As we have seen, there are substantial reasons for believing this picture may be in error. If, as now seems likely, there really was a prehistoric civilisation, it is clear that some of its technology was inherited by the Egyptians. Moses himself, the traditional author of the Torah, was a member of the Egyptian priesthood, hence an initiate of the Egyptian Mysteries.

I have pointed out elsewhere,[42] that the terms 'initiate' and 'priest' have a special meaning when applied to ancient Egypt. The reality is that an Egyptian priest was far more like an astronomer-scientist than a religious mystic, so that whatever his credentials as a prophet of God, Moses was also involved in the transmission of a *scientific* tradition that may well have reached back via Egypt to Atlantis.

Did this tradition enable him to add cipher to the scriptures he presented to the Children of Israel? Although the Torah Code requires computers to break it, there is as yet no suggestion that computers would have been necessary to generate it. But emerging subtleties may yet hint that the original encoding required a

---

[42] In *Martian Genesis*, Piatkus Books, London, 1998.

sophistication – and possibly even mechanical help – far in excess of anything described in Plato's Atlantis.

But if the code is indeed an Atlantean survival, what of its predictive element? To ascribe this glibly to divine intervention simply replaces one mystery with another and, more importantly, ignores modern discoveries about the nature of Time.

Although most of us live as if time were somehow apart from the universe, a sort of river along which everything flows, Einstein's Relativity Theory indicates this is not so. Time is an aspect of Space – or rather, both Time and Space are aspects of a single structure known as Spacetime. Today's physicists have shown experimentally that Time is not absolute. It slows down as an object gains momentum and stops altogether at light speed (the theoretical limit of acceleration). We also know in theory how to build a time machine, although we do not have the technology to construct one in practice.[43] At the sub-atomic level it has been observed that certain particles distort Time and some actually move backwards in Time.

Against this strictly scientific background, the predictive elements of the Torah Code are distinctly less eerie (and arguably less in need of a religious explanation) than might at first appear to be the case. But their implications are no less startling. For if the Torah Code was the result of Atlantean knowledge, that lost civilisation had a far better handle on Time than we do. They were able to use their knowledge to forecast the future.

---

[43] For a full discussion of these fascinating themes, see my *Time Travel: a New Perspective*, published by Llewellyn, USA, 1997.

INDEX

Abraham 119
Africa 2, 3, 5, 44, 45, 66, 120, 126, 128, 168
    Great Rift Valley 45, 91, 164
Agassiz, Louis 69, 70–1, 72, 79, 185, 187
agriculture 9–10, 17, 25, 42, 121, 191
aircraft 18, 194
Alaska 78, 93–4, 101, 112
Americas 2, 5, 24–7, 41–2, 44, 90, 96, 100, 104, 120
anaesthetics 44
ancestors 6–7, 8, 12, 60
Antarctica 4, 56, 82, 112–13
antimatter 148–9
antimony 35
Arab scholarship 55–6
Aratake, Kihachiro 47
architecture 191–2
Arctic 95, 112, 113, 115
arrowheads 13, 94, 190
Assyria 40–1, 132, 133
asteroids 128–9, 134–6, 137, 138–9, 141–2, 145, 146
astronomy 106–8, 127–30, 133–9, 147, 148–51, 152, 155
    ancient 107–8, 131–3, 159–62, 194–5
    see also planets
Athens 5, 6, 13–14, 97, 122
Atlantic Ocean 2, 4–5, 98–9, 118
Atlantis 1–5, 13, 14–18, 56, 159, 193–4
    destruction of 6, 97, 122, 193
Australia 11, 51, 96, 118, 120, 188
Australopithecus 6
Azores 91, 98, 118
Aztecs 19–21, 26, 107

Babylon 42, 107, 119, 131, 132–3, 144, 184, 195
Bacon, Francis 2
Bahamas 4
Bering Strait 8–9, 24, 113
Beth She'arim 41
Bible 39, 40, 110, 169–75, 176, 185, 189
'Bible Code' 195–200
Bode's Law 133–4, 136

Bolivia 2, 22–4
Brazil 3, 96
Brewster, David 41
Bronze Age 17
burial sites 13

calendars 20, 194–5
canals 15, 20, 27, 45
Canary Islands 8, 91, 118
caves 43, 61–2, 96
    animal remains 94–7
    art 62–6
Cayce, Edgar 3, 193
Chad craters 126
cheese-making 43
China 12, 91, 92, 96, 101, 117, 120, 168
climate 109–10, 116
clothes 42, 189
coal 112
comets 125–6, 130, 136, 141, 143, 145, 149, 152, 156
Constantinople 56
copper mining 44
coral 112
Cremo, Michael A. 42
Crete 2, 41, 52–4, 55, 95
Cro-Magnons 7–8
Crowder, T.R. 49
crystal-based technology 193, 194

Dawson, Charles 76–7
Dee, John 2
de Sautuola, Marcelino 62
Dilmun 111
diorite 34
Djebel Sahaba 13

Earth 158–9, 163–4, 177–8
    axis 106, 108, 115, 116, 122, 123–4, 131
    effect of Vela-F 162–92
    orbit 106, 144, 163
    rotation speed 144–5
earthquakes 6, 97, 99–101, 170–1, 175
earthworks 26–7
Egypt, ancient 5, 29–38, 107, 111, 122, 123, 159, 160, 191–2, 199
    maritime travel 51–2
    priest of Sais 123, 124

engineering skills 19–20, 26–7, 31–4, 45–9, 51–2, 191
erratics 67–8, 79, 81, 84–5, 117, 167–8, 180
Eskimo culture 60, 120
extinctions 93–7, 117, 122, 126–7, 187–8

Fawcett, P.H. 3
Fiji 118, 120
fingerprints 43
flint 190
flood 6, 118–21, 176–84
Forbes, Allan, Jr 49
France 12, 28, 43
    caves 44, 64, 66

Germany 64, 68, 69
Gibraltar 3, 4, 5, 56, 95
Golden Age 110–11, 145
granite 35
Greek mythology 111, 120, 123–4
Greenland 82, 112, 113

Haggadah 181
Han Hei, Great 91, 92, 117
Hapgood, Charles 54–6, 57, 170, 192
Heer, Oswald 72, 88, 112
Helios 123–4
Herodotus 30
Herschel, William 134
Hesiod 111
Hindu myths 111, 120, 194
Hipparchus 131, 132
Hodges, Peter 29, 30
Homer 111
Hopewell culture 25–6
horse, domesticated 16, 44

ice, physics of 81–3
Ice Age 7, 8–9, 14, 17, 24, 26, 54–7, 58–66, 114, 184–92
    early theories 67–75
    evidence against 78–83
Iceland 113, 120
Imhotep 191–2
Indians, American 25, 167–8, 180, 181–2, 188
Ipiutak 45
Iran 45, 111
Iraq 10, 40, 121

Ireland 2, 28
iron smelting 44
irrigation 23, 27, 45
Islands of the Blest 111

Japan 43, 47–8, 64
    earthquakes 100–1
Jericho 39–40
Jupiter 125–6, 134, 138, 142, 144,
    145, 156

Kashmir 89, 91–2
Kevkenes Dagh 46
Kimura, Masaki 47, 48
Koran 180
Krakatoa 102–3, 186
Kuiper Belt 152–3, 160

Lagrange, Louis 136
Layard, Henry 40–1
Lebanon 28
libraries, ancient 55, 132
Little Sole Bank 1
Lyell, Charles 70

Madeira 118
Maimon, Rabbi Moses ben
    (Maimonides) 196
Malta 28, 44, 95
mammoths 93, 114, 116–17, 186,
    187–8
Manetho 37
manganese mining 44
Maoris 52, 120, 169
maps, ancient 43, 55–6
Mars 141–2, 143, 144, 145, 146,
    156–7
Mayans 42
megaliths 28
Mercury 137, 140, 144
Mesopotamia 10, 121, 160
metalworking 17, 53
meteorites 128, 135, 136, 139,
    141, 142, 143, 144, 149,
    167–9, 175
Mexico 19–22, 25, 26, 168
Mid-Atlantic Ridge 98–9
Minoan culture 2, 51–4, 55
Miocene era 113–14
Miocene Ocean 117
Mississippi culture 27
moon 145, 162, 177
    orbit 194–5, 198
Moses 196–7, 199
mountains 85–91, 92, 164, 187

Natufians 43
Neanderthals 7, 8
Neptune 142, 144, 145–6, 153–4,
    161
New Caledonia 44
New Zealand 44, 52, 91, 118, 120,
    169
Nigeria 3
Nimrud 41
Nineveh 40–1, 132
Nippur 119, 132
Noah 118–19, 121, 178, 180
Norse mythology 187
nuclear fusion 148

obelisks 29
oil lamps 43
Olbers, Heinrich 135–6
Oort Cloud 143
optical lenses 41
Ovenden, Michael 136–7, 148, 149

Pacific region 44, 45–6, 50–1, 118,
    187
Palestine 42–3
paradise myths 110–12
Peru 27, 168, 187
Petrie, Flinders 31, 35
Phaethon 123–4, 161
Phoenicians 55
Piazzi, Guiseppe 134–5
Piltdown Man 76–7
Pitcairn Island 50–1
planets 107, 108, 133–8, 140–6,
    147, 148, 152–7
    as gods 159–62, 172
    missing 135–7, 141–4, 148,
    149, 152–3, 156
plant growth 115
Plato 4–6, 13–18, 37, 48, 56,
    97–8, 101, 109, 121, 122–3,
    178–9, 192, 193
Playfair, John 68
Pleistocene era 78, 88–91, 93–6,
    98, 116–17, 118, 121, 144,
    151, 169
Pluto 144, 152–3, 161
Poland 43
Ponape 45
Poseidon 3, 15
pottery 43, 53
precession of the equinoxes 131–2
pregnancy test 42
prehistory 6–10, 11–14, 16–17, 25,
    41–9, 56–7
    see also Ice Age; Pleistocene era
Proctor, Richard 107
Ptah 192
pyramids
    in Americas 21–2
    in Egypt 29–31, 35–6

Reinmuth, Karl Wilhelm 129
Rich, Claudius J. 40
Roche Limit 155
Russia 1, 42

Saturn 142, 144, 145, 155, 156,
    161
Schimper, Karl 69–70
Schoch, Robert 38, 47
Scotland 78–9, 180
sea levels 8–9, 59, 75, 91, 92
Serbia 44
Settegast, Mary 56, 64–5
ships 17
Shoemaker-Levy 9 (comet) 125–6
Shott el Djerid, Tunisia 3
Shuruppak 121
Siberia 75, 78, 94, 113, 114,
    116–17, 120, 186
Sicily 94–5
Sippara 119, 132
Sneferu 36

solar system 137–8, 140–1, 144,
    147, 150, 152
    see also planets
Solon 5, 16, 123, 124
Spain 3, 13, 62, 64
Sphinx, Great 38, 192
Spitzbergen islands 112
Sri Lanka 44–5
Strabo 32
Sumerians 10, 49, 111, 119, 121,
    131, 133, 159
supernovas 137, 150–1
    see also Vela supernova
surgery 43–4
Sweden 8, 85
Switzerland 64, 88
Syria 120

tachylite 98
'tangled point complex' 12–13
Tartessian culture 3
tassili N'Ajjer 66
teachers 190–2
tektites 141
Teller, Edward 148
Tenochtitlan 19–20
Thailand 42
Thera 2
Thompson, Richard L. 42
Tiahuanaco 22–4, 26
Tibet 89, 91
Time, nature of 200
Toltecs 168
Torah Code 196–200
Trimil, Java 12
Turin Papyrus 37
Turkey 12, 41, 42
Tyrrhenia 5

Ubaidians 10
Ukraine 43
Ur 119–20, 133
Uranus 134, 142, 144, 145, 154–5,
    161
Utnapishtim 119

Van Flandern, Ton 136
Vasylivka III 13
Vela supernova 151–92
Venus 140–1, 144
'Venus' figurines 64
Virgil 111
volcanoes 102–5, 164

warfare 5, 13, 159, 162
West, John Anthony 33
wine fermentation 43
Woolley, Leonard 119
World Ocean 178, 186
writing 49

Xisuthros 119
Xitli, Mount 21–2

yoghurt-making 43
Yorkshire, England 95–6
Yucatan 44, 46
Yuma points 94

Zeus 124
zodiac 106–7, 132, 133